Write Free

Write Free

ATTRACTING
THE CREATIVE LIFE

Rebecca Lawton
Jordan E. Rosenfeld

BeijaFlor Books ✿ Glen Ellen, California

Cover painting, "Yarrow Meadow," by Irene Guidici Ehret
Copy editing by Melissa B. Mower

Publisher's Cataloging-in-Publication Data
(provided by Quality Books, Inc.)

Lawton, Rebecca, 1954-
Write free : attracting the creative life / by
Rebecca Lawton and Jordan E. Rosenfeld.
p. cm.
Includes bibliographical references.
LCCN 2007940538
ISBN-13: 978-0-9661867-8-9
ISBN-10: 0-9661867-8-8

1. Creation (Literary, artistic, etc.) 2. New
thought.   I. Rosenfeld, Jordan E., 1974- II. Title.
BF408.L39 2008   153.3'5
QBI07-600313

BeijaFlor Books   ✿   Glen Ellen, California
an imprint of Kulupi Press
www.kulupi.com

Printed in the United States of America
with soy-based ink on
30% post-consumer content paper
1 2 3 4 5 6 7 8 9 0

Dedicated to Jennie Landfield,
whose vision of this book preceded ours
and encouraged it into being.

CONTENTS

Acknowledgments   11

Introductions   13

CLEARING

Letting Go   21

Accentuating the Positive   35

Feeling Better   45

REVISING

Unleashing Your Desires   63

If You Know It, You Can Change It   73

Living Your Story   85

FEELING YOUR STORY

Feelings Create Our Reality   101

Quick Tricks to Positivity   113

The Write Way   123

WRITING FREE!

Wishing and Hoping   137

Engaging Your Desire   145

Allowing Your Good   155

Suggested Reading   165

About the Authors   167

ACKNOWLEDGMENTS

Although we came to the idea of Write Free and the power of attraction spontaneously, we owe great inspiration and appreciation to Lynn Grabhorn, author of *Excuse Me, Your Life is Waiting* (Hampton Roads), and Esther and Jerry Hicks, authors of *Ask and It is Given* (Hay House). Grateful thanks to writers Ana Manwaring, Elizabeth Rose, Rhiannon Fionn, Christie Collins, and Philip Beard for contributing their personal accounts. Their stories inspire us!

A Word from Rebecca Lawton

My first exposure to the natural laws governing forces of attraction must have been while reading Sir Isaac Newton's work in physics. Bodies in motion exert influence over other bodies, he wrote. "If anyone presses a stone with a finger, the finger is also pressed by the stone." Newton demonstrated with experiments a variety of forces he could neither see nor fully explain. He asked that his propositions be "read with an open mind" and that readers continue their own inquiries into the workings of the universe. Newton himself drew a distinction between physical experiences ("derived from phenomena through the five external senses") and metaphysical (not perceptible through sight, smell, sound, touch, or taste).

For many years, Jordan and I have enjoyed careers planted more firmly in the physical realm than the metaphysical. Jordan, as a journalist, has followed rigorous protocols when interviewing her subjects for articles in newspapers and magazines. I, as a scientist, have learned to be precise when observing and describing the workings of the earth. We both owe much to our professional experiences accurately witnessing life on this planet. But we are also authors of poetry and fiction, and we're quite capable of creating worlds in which we ask our readers to suspend disbelief while being transported to other worlds and realities.

When Jordan and I discovered the metaphysical principles of attraction, we knew we'd found a life force as invisible and undeniable as gravity. We thought it was just by chance that we'd done so, until we looked a little closer at both our paths leading to that place and time. We'd both been writers for years—in fact, we met through our mutual writer's community in northern California. We'd both adhered to daily writing practices, shared our love for story in workshops and writing groups, and lived our individual versions of the writer's life. Looking back, our paths to the power of attraction wove clearly through the very creative and marvelously tangled portions of our literary lives.

Attracting the creative life relies on a universal principle in which like attracts like: all beings vibrate energy that attracts other, similar energy. When we use our writing energy to consciously attract the lives we want, we're flowing our creative vibrations onto paper. In keeping with the principle of attraction, it's no wonder that Jordan and I found each other and quickly formed a professional partnership. We were astounded at how writing could be a powerful force in other aspects of our lives as well. We began to look for examples of its effectiveness. The results of our search are presented in this book.

We invite you to investigate the principles of the unseen world on your own, in as much depth as you'd like. In the back of this book, we recommend further reading about writing, the metaphysical world, and attracting your ideal life. Some authors have gone beyond the scope of this book to explain how vibrational metaphysics work. We hope you'll explore some of these sources. However, we believe that, no matter how deep your own investigation into laws of attraction, the activities we've designed herein will improve your life. They are especially suited to writers and other inspired souls.

We may never completely understand our inner lives. To Newton's caveat to read with an open mind, we can only add "and with an open heart." Our wish is that these pages conspire to achieve your fullest living—and writing—now.

Write Free

A Word from Jordan E. Rosenfeld

Welcome fellow writer and artistic soul! You create worlds, express ideas, record moments of great beauty, and evoke emotional depth and intellectual curiosity with your creative gifts. Yours is not a small charge. You have the power of persuasion: the means to move, transform, and reach those who come in contact with your words and your art. The fact that you are holding this book in your hands means you have decided to take your creative life seriously.

Rebecca and I began to write this book in the spirit of sharing powerful, life-changing information with other writers who also feel the pull of the creative during a day at work, or when driving down the road, or when tending to such necessary things as doing laundry. As we developed this book, however, it became clear to us that the distinction between writers and other types of artists is not so wide, and though we come at this work as writers and lean toward writers in our discussions, the activities in our book are designed for anyone pursuing a creative life.

The two of us know what it is like to dream of creating while doing other things, to long for a fulfilling artistic life only to feel frustrated because practical details come between the urge and the action. Yet we were dedicated to carving out the artistic life we knew we could have, if only we could find the right path. Through joyful play we stumbled onto a form for energizing our dreams, a method for actively attracting our desires that impressed us so much that we simply could not keep it to ourselves. Just as you create worlds, images, essays, and stories, you can create the artist's life you dream of with just as much pleasure and delight.

The secret is so simple that it is revolutionary. You have an advantage in this game of actively creating the artistic life you want. You are already good at identifying your thoughts and feelings through words. You already have the perfect technology at your disposal for seeing clearly and having exactly what you want: Your writing! Your creative talent will lead you to your desires, and all we ask is that you feel good while doing it.

"Write Free" has two meanings to us. First, we use it to mean writing in an open-minded, openhearted state of consciousness. To Write Free is to cover the page with words and to let your creativity be unleashed. Editing and criticism can come later. Second, we believe it expresses the state of writing our deepest desires, as we have done in this book's activities, to create better, freer lives. If you can actively feel good for just a minute each day, and playfully engage the activities, suggestions, and ideas in this book, we are confident that you will see your artistic life move from a dream to a reality.

We feel so great that you picked up this book. Happy creating!

PART ONE

CLEARING

Freeing your life of unwanted feelings

Today there are special instruments that can find our exact location on the planet based on satellite signals. These special instruments—Global Positioning System, or GPS, units—tell us where we are, which way we're going, and how far we've come from our starting point.

In our lives we all have our own inner topography based on our experiences. Often we need to take our own bearings to chart a course through not only the many obstacles but also the delicious options life gives us. In choosing our way, we can consult with our own versions of a GPS unit. The wonderful lesson to be learned is that the unit is already built into us—call it our internal compass—that's based on our feelings. The combination of experience and these guiding feelings is extremely powerful.

Feelings are amazingly potent forces. They color our outlook and determine the character of our days. Feelings range from the sublime to the unbearable, from opaque darkness to bright light.

Much of the metaphysical literature says that a few seconds of pure, focused feeling creates an emotional environment that attracts a corresponding physical experience. We like to be generous and give the feelings a full minute to do their work. Understanding feelings, however—and clearing out unwanted ones—requires knowing what they are. Sounds simple, but like anything in life, it requires practice. In Part One, we invite you to begin focusing on the feelings that are already shaping your experience. The first step toward getting what you want in life is to get rid of *feelings* that you don't want. Part One will guide you through activities that help free your life of unwanted feelings.

Write Free

CHAPTER ONE

Letting Go

I believe the very purpose of life is to achieve happiness.

—The Dalai Lama

Rebecca writes:

Immediately after Jordan and I discovered the benefit of intentionally focusing feelings on our own writing lives, we wanted to share it with other writers. We also wanted to teach what we'd learned while surrounded by nature. Being in a beautiful, peaceful setting had enhanced our own ability to absorb the first lessons of the power of attraction. We wanted others to experience this power as well.

We contacted our favorite retreat center on the beautiful Navarro River in Mendocino County. The place has fabulous meals, a quiet location ideally suited to creative work, and a view of a forested ridge with constantly changing, inspiring light. The retreat center had weekend space for a group of twenty or so in late May—just three months away.

We knew that three months wasn't a lot of lead time to get the word out, but we took a leap of faith and reserved the weekend. First we paid a deposit that would hold the facility. Next we invited special presenters who we knew exemplified the writer's life. Finally, we prepared our own talks about the power of attraction. When we felt we had everything in place, we advertised the weekend.

Although we hadn't held such a retreat before, we focused our energy on an outcome in which a full complement of participants would share a weekend of retreat and writing with us. If, during the weekend, we could communicate how to Write Free to those participants, we'd feel we had succeeded. We kept our focus on a very specific, very positive outcome, because if we failed, we'd lose a lot of money and plenty of credibility.

Sign-ups for the weekend trickled in from around the state and across the country. Soon half the openings had filled. Then, just as quickly as they'd started ringing, the phones stopped. No more sign-ups showed up in our e-mail in-boxes and post office boxes. We were nowhere near critical mass and considered canceling the weekend. Then the two of us realized what had happened—we'd taken our focus off the weekend and let our energy flag. We'd allowed failure to become an option.

Jordan and I regrouped. Keeping our attention off any anxiety about numbers and shifting back to the success of the weekend itself, we also transformed our energy. Sign-ups resumed flowing in, all the way up until the day of the retreat.

When the two of us arrived at the retreat and heads had been counted, we had the number of participants we'd hoped for. We went on to share an astounding and transforming weekend in which the writers let themselves write their intentions as artists. The successes of everyone who participated are still being revealed and celebrated daily.

Feelings are the capital in which writers and other artists trade. We're often called to express emotion in our work, whether it's assigning the motive of anger to a fictional character or using paint to express joy on canvas. For any artist, conveying feelings in an identifiable way can make the difference between producing a piece that is simply well wrought and one that pulses with authentic life. Writers and other artists already know to engage their feelings as they touch pens to paper, brushes to easel, fingers to instruments, and feet to the studio floor.

Feelings are also foundational in working with principles of attraction, which tell us that as we feel, we attract. To get what we want in life, it's essential that we feel the sensations associated with already having it. It's like taking a walk to a favorite place. You have your destination in mind: maybe you're strolling to your favorite deli and you can already taste the sweet slices of tomato on the sandwich you'll order when you arrive. Or you're headed to a lake in a mountain clearing, and as you ramble among the fir and pine, you can imagine how it will feel to kick off your boots and dip your feet into the bracing water. Those sensations draw you forward on the path as surely as night follows day.

The guiding feeling on your journey, though, is to know you'll arrive. You set out with no doubts in your mind, you have your scribbled directions, and you're full of confidence that you'll reach your destination. You even arrive so soon you wish you'd savored the journey more fully. With a positive outlook steering your course, you can't help but choose the right path to reach your heart's desire.

In this chapter you'll experiment with the most basic building blocks in your creative toolkit—your feelings—and learn how they serve to get you where you're going. Although most people believe they know the difference between a positive and negative feeling, this chapter will help you identify not only what you're feeling in the moment but also how to raise your bad feelings to good any time you're ready. You'll feel the sensation of turning rejection to triumph, fear to confidence, pain to joy, all while sitting anywhere—your writer's corner, your artist's studio, the local café—with pen in hand.

ACTIVITIES

✍ Hard Times

Remember a time when you felt hurt, lost, or rejected? You may have received bad news, for example, or had an accident, or experienced conflict with a loved one. Your feelings at such times may have been anger, sorrow, guilt, or some other negative emotion. No doubt your impulse was to work through these feelings as quickly as possible to get them behind you. Pushing away bad feelings is a natural urge, but looking at hard times in your past can be instructive. We'll do it here just long enough to learn the value of understanding how we *felt* during these key past experiences.

I. Create two columns numbered 1 through 10 along the left side of a fresh page in your journal. Beside each number write a key phrase from a difficult time in your past. The negative events can be large or small.

Example: *Hard Times*

1. *When mom died*

2. *When our cat ran off*

3. *During my divorce*

4. *My bout with the flu last week*

II. In the right column, write the dominant negative feeling you can recall from hard time number 1. Stop after the first one!

Example: 1. *When mom died*   *Lonely*

III. Now close your eyes and allow yourself a minute to remember how that time felt. Take a quick trip to the dark side. As writers, we're often reminded to show, not tell, how things feel. Show yourself the details of your hard time. Put yourself back in that dim room; recall the closed curtains. Is there a face with a hurt expression, a sad song on the radio that you'll never forget? Let yourself get into that old sensation, deep in the emotional center of your being. Try to stop at fifteen seconds, and definitely go no longer than thirty seconds.

IV. On the next page in your journal, in big letters, write possible antonyms for the dominant negative emotion. Start with "*I feel loved when I think of . . .*" or "*I feel better when I remember . . .* " You may reach back farther than the hard time to find a pleasurable emotion, you may remember something from just yesterday, or you may anticipate the future. This is your chance to dig for vocabulary. When you write a word that rings your positive-feeling bell, go directly into writing that builds on the emotion. Write for at least a minute without stopping, always moving the hand, until you feel a lift in your spirit for at least a minute.

Example: *Lonely*

Antonyms: *CONNECTED, TOGETHER, JOINED, UNITED, LOVED...DING!*

Freewrite: *I feel loved when I think of all the days my mother took care of me, holding me, listening to my stories, making her sympathetic face. I can still hear her voice when she read to me—she made me feel warm, connected, and protected. I have good memories of listening to records she bought me, sitting on the floor of the living room, my mother in the kitchen baking peanut butter cookies . . .*

V. Go back to your list and work through the remaining hard times, listing first the negative emotion and then writing the emotional context of the positive experience.

You may want to spend days doing this activity. Go at your own pace—delving into the feelings associated with hard times may take a while. Notice how you are able to pull yourself out of the painful feelings just by connecting your hand to the page and conjuring up opposite emotions. You don't have to leave your chair. It isn't necessary to travel around the world, find a new lover, or get a raise at work to feel better. Notice that you have the power to change a negative emotion to a positive one—on your own! Good feelings are ever available to you, as freely given as the oxygen in fresh air. To Write Free is to resonate in accordance with them, speeding them your way!

<u>Some tips</u>: It's important that you always end this game (and those that follow) on a positive note. The good feelings raise your vibration and attract more of the same. Remember to spend at least a minute in the positive emotion, enough time to align with similar good feelings in the atmosphere around you.

✍ The Circle of Lack

What is lack? It's the sense that we don't have enough of something. It's normal and natural to bemoan lack, but it's also good to remember that it's a feeling state that can be changed. For this game, we'll identify (1) what we believe we don't have enough of AND (2) what we want to have in greater quantities in our lives!

I. Draw a big circle in your notebook. This is your Circle of Lack. Divide it into eight equal sections, like the slices of a pie cut to share with eight equally hungry guests. In the bottom four sections, write phrases to complete the sentence, "I don't have . . ."

Example: *I don't have . . .*

1.   *Enough money*

2.   *A boyfriend*

3.   *Enough help around the house*

4.   *A literary agent*

II. Outside the pie, or on the opposite page, scribble the reasons you believe you don't have lack number one. When you come upon the belief that rings true for you, stop.

Example: *I don't have...*

1.   *Enough money*

I don't have enough money because . . . money doesn't grow on trees, the economy is terrible, my bank pays lousy interest, I need a better job, I need a raise at work, I'm not doing what I love to do and money isn't flowing to me . . . Ding!

III. Write the reason in the top section of the pie, opposite lack number one.

Example: *I would have enough money if . . .*

1.   *I was doing what I loved to do and money flowed to me.*

IV. Close your eyes and allow yourself at least a minute to feel the fullness of the emotion associated with HAVING that situation or thing on the top half of the pie.

Let your feelings run wild. Feel the sensation of making

all the money you need and want. Don't worry if it hasn't happened already; don't worry about taking the steps to make it happen. Just allow yourself to feel the sensation of taking a whopping big check to the bank, endorsing it with your favorite pen, and seeing your name on the line that follows "Pay to the Order of."

V. Go back to the remaining slices of the pie. Repeat the above steps for each slice of the Circle of Lack.

Some tips: This is your chance to explore the reasons you believe you experience lack. It's also your chance to turn a Circle of Lack into a big, juicy, scrumptious pie! As you dig into this game, let yourself feel the details of the opposite, positive experience for each of your lacks: the exercise in which you have everything your heart desires. Your writer's imagination can really help with the sensory experience associated with your desires. Your training in choosing just the right metaphor or setting the perfect scene will help you here. Explore your beliefs about lack with confidence. You won't need them much longer—you may allow them to fall away, as a lizard sheds its skin.

✍ My Favorite Things

It's often easier to focus on things you dislike than it is naming those you like. For example: Your child is having trouble at school with a group of unfriendly peers. It's easy to see the situation as all negative: you might recall your own difficulties at a similar age and remember your tormentors less than fondly. You might forget that, because of the discomfort of that time, you began keeping a daily journal that led to your becoming a writer.

We have a friend named Jimmy who, many years ago, left home to join the traveling circus at the age of fifteen. To fit in with his new, rough crowd, Jimmy quickly took up smoking cigarettes, drinking, and swearing like the carnival worker he'd become. He had to labor long hours to keep up with the more experienced carnies—they were hard muscled, opinionated specialists with no time to mentor a teenaged boy. Jimmy worked hard, for longer hours than he thought possible, because he wanted the experience of roaming the country with colorful, itinerant workers. He'd fled an ordinary suburban life and found himself among people who had better stories than he'd ever read in the books back home.

It was difficult at first, but with time Jimmy found his hands toughening to the work, his mind finding answers to challenges such as how to get the elephant tent up in a driving rainstorm with only one other worker to help, and his heart opening up to the sights, sounds, and smells of the carnival. In six months, after turning sixteen, he had become a crew chief, a specialist in entourage logistics.

At the age of twenty-one, Jimmy decided he'd had enough of the circus and made his way back home. His little suburb seemed as quiet as ever, but he no longer chafed at its tameness. He had experiences under his belt to last a lifetime—and a litany of stories to record. He opened an independent bookstore and took up writing, fed by the tales he'd lived while on the road. The night the fat lady couldn't get out the door of her trailer? Great fodder for a short story. The lost lions in the red rock country of northern Arizona? A wonderful children's book.

Jimmy is now a successful author, a happy entrepreneur in his hometown, and the father of two energetic preteen boys. Would he ever let them join the circus? No way, he says. But after thinking a while, he remembers

Write Free

that as difficult as life was on the road, he grew into it and matured much faster than he ever could have at home. "It was worth the sacrifices," he says. "The missed days at high school, the growing up too fast. The hardest times led to the richest memories. I suppose protecting my boys from everything keeps them from really living."

In this game, you get to cite your least favorite things as a means of understanding how they lead to your favorite things.

I. Designate another two-column page in your note-book. Again, number the rows from 1 to 10 in both columns, this time filling the left column with some of your current least favorite things.

Example: *Least favorite things*

    1. *Dad's diagnosis*

    2. *Pinging noise in car engine*

    3. *Bullies at school*

    4. *Uninsured drivers*

II. In the right column, write the dominant feeling associated with least favorite thing number 1. Stop after the first one!

Example: *Least favorite things*

    1. *Dad's diagnosis*   *Helpless*

III. Now close your eyes and allow yourself a minute to feel the fullness of the emotion.

Lean into the feeling. Let yourself feel the details. Allow your writer's imagination to carry you as deep as it will. Try to stop after fifteen seconds of continuous feeling, and definitely go no longer than thirty seconds.

IV. On the next page in your journal, complete as many of the following sentences as you can about the situation regarding your least favorite thing.

One good thing about...

The nicest thing I can say about...

*If I had to pick something I liked about _____,
it would be . . .*

My favorite thing about _____ is...

Example: *Least favorite things*

   1.   *Dad's diagnosis*   *Helpless*

One good thing about Dad's diagnosis is now we know why he's been in pain. The nicest thing I can say about Dad's diagnosis is that the doctors told us about it quickly. If I had to pick something I liked about Dad's diagnosis, it would be that he received the news when we could be with him. My favorite thing about Dad's diagnosis is that it's not as bad as we thought it would be.

V. When you finish playing with the first thing on your list, repeat it using a different least favorite thing.

Don't rush. Keep going until you feel your attitude shift from a negative to positive perspective and can hold it there for a minute.

VI. Go back and continue through the remaining least favorite things, taking them at your own speed and one at a time.

<u>Some tips</u>: It's important to note that, while you may not feel great about a situation, using these other techniques, you can begin to feel better. That's an important step to take toward feeling good. Again, take your time playing this game and, when you come to a positive emotion, remember to spend at least a minute feeling it. It's not the thought that counts; it's the feeling!

CHAPTER TWO

Accentuating the Positive

Tell me, what is it you plan to do
with your one wild and precious life?

— Mary Oliver

Rebecca writes:

I'd been trying to place my work with the editor of a personal essay column in a large metropolitan newspaper. My submissions had been rejected repeatedly, even though I knew my style was right for the column. The first few essays were returned with a simple, "No, thanks," but by the fifth or sixth submission they were returned with the comment, "I'm not interested." I took this remark personally, and I stopped submitting to the column altogether. I even did the unacceptable. I wrote a terse, "I get the message—have a great life" return e-mail to the editor. I was convinced that that particular market was closed to me.

I mentioned the above series of events to Jordan in one of our regular telephone conferences in which we refresh the principles of Write Free. She suggested I submit again, to the same editor, but this time using a *nom de plume*. We agreed that by letting go of my identity as someone who would never be published in that column, I would soften the insistent feeling that was working against me.

I wrote another personal essay, in part with the column in mind but mostly with the intention of simply telling my story. There was a message I wanted to convey in the piece: one of loss and sadness, but also of triumph and survival. Because I had taken my focus off publication while writing, I went deep into storytelling mode. Much of the writing for the piece was done in subconscious writing fashion. When I finished a decent draft, I went outside to water my flower garden. I felt a certainty that hadn't been there before. The essay was so good, so moving, I knew it would be published—if not in the target column, then certainly elsewhere.

The next morning, after a final read-through, I sent the essay to the newspaper column using a *nom de plume* I'd made up the night before. Within hours the editor had accepted it, scheduled it for publication, and let me know she'd prefer that I use my real name as the byline. The previous curse of rejections had been broken, and I'm convinced it was due to letting go and allowing deeper, more creative work to flow.

In Chapter One, you identified what you don't want— hard times, feelings of lack, least favorite things. Now you can go about letting them go. Again this process is helped by the fact that you're a writer. You create worlds every day by choosing one word over another, one point of view, one genre in which to write. In this chapter, we're simply asking you to make the same choices for your feelings: what mood will you release so you can choose another? With you as the protagonist, how will it feel to lead your supporting characters? In what setting will you act out your "wild and precious life"?

You may think the four winds of fate determine the

Write Free

direction your life goes, and the environment does bear on your experience, but it's your feelings that determine the choices you make in your environment. Making choices involves constantly deciding what you want so you can let go of what doesn't suit you. For this type of decision making, no guide is more important than your inner compass, that bundle of feelings that is always present in your own psyche.

When we first learned about the power of attraction, we worked very hard at learning how to raise our positive vibrations to attract our good. We studied the literature dealing with attracting our best lives, labored through exercises in workbooks, and had many discussions about what seemed to be working (i.e., what increased our ease and abundance). One missing piece, though, was that we were still holding on to enough low-vibration or negative perspectives to counter all the positive work we were doing.

The power of the negative to block your good is overwhelming. But you have power, too: choice.

Just as you choose the right line enjambment for a poem, or the most fitting name for a short story or essay, you can choose not to go to the negative places that destroy your good.

It may sound like a lot of work—making choices and being deliberate with your feelings—but you're flowing your energy anyway, often in unconscious ways that sabotage the ease of your life and put up barriers. It's better to have awareness of what you're doing and understand how you're affecting your life. Remember, just a minute of focused good vibration can change your world. You're in charge of letting go of your don't wants, and you—guided by your feelings—can make choices that allow everything and everyone around you to play their supportive roles in your amazingly wild, precious, and abundant life story.

ACTIVITIES

✍ Choosing Language

Language is the heart and soul of writing. Choosing the proper language to describe your life is an important part of living well. Vocabulary and perspective, building blocks of language, are no less powerful in life than they are in literature. Think of the plucky voice of Huckleberry Finn and his amazing adventures; the survivor's view of Ishmael in *Moby Dick*; the openhearted optimism of Jo in *Little Women*. The language of these protagonists had much to do with where they went in life.

Try the following game to help choose the language you'll use during your time on Earth.

I. Write a sentence that accurately describes an unwanted situation you're currently facing.

> Example: *Our kitchen remodel has become too*
> *costly to complete.*

II. Next, write a second sentence that intensifies your feelings associated with sentence number one.

> Example: *The designer and contractor never*
> *paid attention to what we wanted.*

In this example, you may have begun your kitchen remodel project with a certain budget in mind. You even told your designer and contractor the budget amount, but the job is now twice what you'd projected and giving you fits. You write a few more sentences that don't shy away from your most negative feelings about the situation.

Write Free

Example: *The designer and contractor are just creating more work for themselves. All of the vendors are holding out their hands for more money on this job.*

III. Now, consciously make a shift. Write a few sentences associated with any positive feelings you might have about the subject. They don't have to be happy-go-lucky yet, but try to reach for something better:

> *Even if they haven't listened to everything we've said, the contractor and designer really are "can-do."* (better)

> *The new kitchen will be beautiful.* (better)

> *The kitchen will be comfortable year round—warm in winter, cool in summer—with all the new appliances.* (good)

> *We'll finally be able to entertain more than one dinner guest at a time!* (great)

Notice how your feelings shift as you choose to let go of your bleakest thoughts. Can you sense the change from dark to light, down to up, heavy to buoyant? That shift is something within your power. You can change your feelings any time you wish.

Once you change the language, you may just find the situation no longer presents the same challenges. Writing your situation in a new light allows you to stay with the new, positive feelings long enough to let them do their work. Remember, a minute is all it takes to change a bad situation. Once the vibrations you're generating are higher and more positive, you'll notice the circumstances around you changing. Support in the form of money, opportunity, and ideas will flow in your direction. Finding the support is the universe's role, not yours—your job is to begin to attract your good simply by describing a situation using more positive language. Your new perspective can indeed change the energy of your world.

Some tips: Try journaling about your perspective on a situation during times of both negative and positive feelings. A written record of your life changing for the better is a powerful testimony to the strength of your personal role in the quality of your life. Returning to the journal entries in future days will also lift your vibrations!

✍ The Power of Ten

Releasing negative feelings that cause low vibrations isn't the only way we can let go of what no longer serves us. Similarly, material possessions carry energy that reflects our feeling state. We can choose to keep this feeling state by hanging on to possessions longer than needed.

Removing clutter from our homes is a well-known method of letting go of old thought processes and patterns of living. But we writers have our own special forms of clutter associated with our craft: old rejection letters from publishers, multiple drafts of stories long since published and "finished," our grandmother's writing desk that we've sworn we'll use someday that is now collecting dust in the garden shed.

There are many good books on clearing clutter for renewed energy in the home and office, and we list a few in the Suggested Reading section at the end of this book. But you can begin to clear out your writer's clutter by adopting the following practice as a regular part of your writing life. Sometime when you're suffering from writer's block, boredom, or are simply in need of a break, try the Power of Ten method and see what happens.

I. Select a pile of clutter on your desk or in a single manila folder in your writer's file.

Example: *The stack of papers to my left needs sorting.*

II. Pull your recycling bin up close and personal. Pick a single sheet of paper from the file and, without hesitating, question whether you need to keep it. If not, recycle it.

Example: *Does this object serve a positive purpose? Is it necessary that I keep it? Am I being kind to myself by holding on to it?*

III. Repeat this exercise with nine other objects or sheets of paper. Start by processing no more than ten objects at a time.

Feel how much lighter you become with every load of unneeded paper or item that leaves your file and home. Allow yourself to be in a feeling state as you lighten your clutter into manageable bites, just ten items at a time. Allow yourself to let go of old pieces of paper that send a jolt of negative feelings through you each time you handle them.

Keep only those entities that serve you now.

Some tips: The hardest part of this exercise is to release those things given us by some beloved relative or friend. Just remember there's no need to rush the release of old letters and objects associated with positive times in your life. Let them go when you're ready. Know that when you do you're releasing not only any stuck energy you might have invested in the object, you're also releasing the stuckness of the person, living or dead, who gave you the object in the first place.

✍ Getting Physical

Physical activity and effort are often thought of as the realm of athletes. Writers and other artistic souls generally excuse themselves from exertion, from being good with their bodies, and from having keen hand-to-eye coordination. However, although it might sound elementary to say so, feelings are physical sensations. They are as much related to our bodies as bike riding, playing hoops, and swimming. A feeling is a gut sense, visceral awareness, or quickening in the heart. Giving attention to what we're feeling at any moment is tuning into a physical state and, like other physical activities, requires practice.

Getting physical, acting out the way we want to *feel*, can be a challenge for writers and other inspired souls, but it's part of being whole. What we're asking for in this activity is your participation in connecting with the physical part of your being that generates feelings.

I. In your journal, list four beliefs you hold about yourself that you'd like to release.

Examples: 1. *I'm too fat.*

             2. *I'm too shy.*

             3. *I'll never publish that one story.*

             4. *I'll never capture the attention of an editor.*

II. Next, stand up. Face your favorite direction in the room—an open window or a wall with a beloved painting or photograph. Focus your attention in your solar plexus. Start with your first belief.

Example: *I'm too fat.*

Being overweight feels heavy, lethargic, and ponderous. If you were to give into this emotion, you'd lumber around the room, experiencing the full weight of your emotions related to feeling too fat.

III. Now call up the opposite feeling.

Example: *I'm just the right weight.*

What is your ideal weight? What would it take for you to feel you're just right in terms of this belief? How much would you weigh? Think of an exact number. How would you look? See yourself in that old dress you love or a new pair of jeans.

IV. Physically act the opposite of that which you want to change.

Feel the sensation of being light. Dance around the room. Feel the body you want for living this life. Feel the buoyancy, the beauty. Let yourself go for as long as you like, but don't stop before you've acted out this positive experience for at least a minute.

Some tips: This is a wonderful activity that works well with the writing-related beliefs on your list. How does it feel to publish that story that's been hard to place? Act it out, from the informed feeling you get while researching the right market for publication, to the excitement of receiving the acceptance letter, to the joy of depositing the check in your bank account. How does it feel to capture the attention of an editor whose work you admire? Act it out, from the validation of receiving the phone call admiring your piece to the pleasure of polishing a sentence or two with her guidance. In creating the scene associated with each one of your heart's desires, you let go of the physical sensations associated with living with the opposite beliefs. Getting physical is a fun way to raise your vibrations and signal the universe just who you are and where you're going.

CHAPTER THREE

Feeling Better

How refreshing!
Moon over this gate through which,
at last, I'm free to pass.

—Issa

Rebecca writes:

Ana, a writing colleague of ours, tells the inspiring story of how her feelings about a dream led her to an unforgettable time in her life. She'd enrolled in a past-life seminar at the local college and was participating in a classroom hypnotic regression. As Ana writes, "The hypnotist intoned, 'Go deeper, back to another time; a time you did something useful. Deeper . . . let the images flow. Deeper—Deeper.' The hypnotist's voice hovered in the ethereal music that filled the classroom where our group had gathered for the seminar. 'Bring something back that will serve your present life,' he said.

"Letting my mind open to the images that appeared, I drifted on the sounds of voice and music. I saw myself atop a pyramid—I was a sculptor carving a white stone. The chatter of parrots echoed up from the dense forest and the sky was an immense blue canopy above me. Chink,

chink—I smelled the dust of hot stone. I was the recorder of events, a writer with my mallet, telling the story of kings and sacrifice.

"Once I 'woke up,' the images, sounds, and smells of the hypnosis lingered vivid and sharp—and they remained for months after. I felt I needed to follow the images to the dreamscape I'd envisioned. But how could I, a bookkeeper, run off to explore jungle ruins? I couldn't afford that kind of trip! Anyway, who has that kind of time?

"But I kept thinking about it. It felt so real. Someday I'd experience the freedom of standing at the top of a pyramid watching toucans glide tree to tree far below me. Of this, I was certain.

"I decided I'd prepare for it. For the next four years, I studied Spanish and ancient Mexican archaeology. I wrote stories about the sculptor. My 'dream' gave me solace when I was down and entertainment when I was bored. I was full of energy and yearning when I remembered my past-life regression. I saw myself in Mexico and Guatemala, exploring decaying cities and writing about it.

"The solution to my dilemma came in an unexpected way. George Bush, Sr., bombed Iraq in early 1991, causing the stock I inherited to jump in value with the wartime bull market. I cashed in. My clients, who were contractors and developers, had no work for me when the real estate market went bust in the aftermath of the war. Time and money were mine! My road was free of obstacles.

"I chugged across the Tucson/Nogales border on July 24, 1991, in my custom outfitted VW pop-up camper ready for an adventure. For two and a half years, I explored Mexico, Belize, and the Petén region of Guatemala. It was the time of my life, a dream made real simply because I never let it go away."

Many feel-good philosophies advise us to make immediate shifts from being in pain to being happy. Many tell us that the way to feel good is to, by god, feel good. Often we think we can pull ourselves up by our bootstraps from bad moods to a state of ecstasy, but just as often we don't. Sometimes we're so down in the dumps that we doubt we'll ever be at our best again, feeling positive and letting go of the negative. When we're in the lows of the artistic doldrums, too, perhaps not writing or painting or otherwise feeling the energy of our dreams, the distance from where we are to where we want to be to feel happy can look so vast, we think we've fallen into some abyss.

The truth is, there are many paths out of the depths. One principle of the power of attraction that serves the artist well is that of feeling better; an intermediate stage we can pass through on our way up from feeling bad to feeling good. It's easier to get out of the lowest of the lows if we aim for a state that simply feels better than where we are now.

Sounds straightforward, and it is. But to pull it off, we need to tune in to our feelings. How am I feeling now? What would feel better? Which emotion has a higher vibration state than another? All of these are good questions.

In Ana's story, she transitioned from feeling a trip was impossible, through a stage of preparation, to the heights of achieving her dream. Along the way, she stayed in touch with her feeling vibrations through writing.

In the activities in this chapter, we'll be referring to The Feeling List, a ranking of emotions from low to high vibration. There are eleven levels on the list and three choices of feelings at each level. We'll be exploring techniques that help move our feeling state up the list from low vibration to high vibration. Explore the list and prepare to have fun with it—after all, it's about feelings, true, but it's also about choosing words—something at which writers excel.

THE FEELING LIST

High Level

1. Joyful/Loved/Free

2. Happy/Eager/Passionate

3. Enthusiastic/Appreciated/Empowered

4. Hopeful/Optimistic/Expectant

5. Content/Accepting/Okay

6. Undecided/Bored/Impatient

7. Frustrated/Pessimistic/Disappointed

8. Worried/Discouraged/Overwhelmed

9. Jealous/Hateful/Blaming

10. Insecure/Guilty/Unworthy

11. Fearful/Depressed/Powerless

Low Level

Write Free

ACTIVITIES

✍ Leveraging

To leverage is to raise or move by use of a lever, which is generally thought of as a pry bar or tool. Leveraging can also be a compelling force. In this game you'll leverage your feelings up a series of levels on The Feeling List. This game is best played when your feeling state could stand a bit of raising, say from Levels 6 through 11, to a higher level, say Levels 1 through 5. The lever you'll be using is the force of writing your emotions.

I. Number five lines in your journal from 1 to 5. List "high," "medium high," "medium," "medium low," and "low" next to the numbers.

Example: 1. *high*

2. *medium high*

3. *medium*

4. *medium low*

5. *low*

II. In a second column, write your current feeling state opposite the appropriate adjective.

Example: 1. *high*

2. *medium high*

3. *medium*

4. *medium low*

5. *low*   *I'm feeling bleak*

III. Now, journal about that feeling state, using it as a prompt for your writing.

Example: *I'm feeling bleak...*

...because I've been sick for a week. The end of summer came, the kids are back in school, and I feel time marching on in a way that makes me feel old. I feel summer flew by before I could appreciate it! It's true that the kids didn't complain about going back to school...

IV.   When you reach a place in your journaling that feels at least a little positive, move the more-positive statement to the appropriate level on your leveraging list.

Example: 1. *high*

2. *medium high*

3. *medium*

4. *medium low*   *The kids didn't complain*

5. *low*   *I'm feeling inexplicably bleak*

V. Then keep writing. Repeat Step III, using the new statement as your writing prompt.

Example: *The kids didn't complain...*

...about going back to school because they were eager to see their friends. Rachel called Lisa and arranged to get together to walk to school, and both kids were content as they left yesterday morning...

VI. Repeat Step IV, moving a new statement to the appropriate level on your leveraging list. Continue the process until you have entries for all five levels.

Example: 1. *high*   *It was a fun summer!*

2. *medium high*   *We had a good final week off.*
3. *medium*   *Both kids were content.*
4. *medium low*   *The kids didn't complain.*
5. *low*   *I'm feeling inexplicably bleak.*

Now look at where you've arrived emotionally from where you've begun: you leveraged yourself from "I'm feeling inexplicably bleak" to "It was a fun summer!" All with the flourish of your pen.

<u>Some tips</u>: Try this game with ten levels, fifteen levels, and on up to twenty. It's a great way to move back and forth between any freewrite and the leveraging list. The list focuses on the positive influence of your journaling. As you play, notice your feelings climbing higher. Don't force them. They'll come as you write. You'll leverage yourself out of your low place—try it and see!

✍ Graphing Game

Writers often have an affinity for words to the exclusion of numbers and diagrams. Often we don't consider the use of graphs and pictures when attempting to communicate. In truth, graphics are amazingly powerful tools for analyzing a problem. This game uses graphics as tools for diagramming your feelings. The graphics may seem too technical to help you understand something as personal as the inner workings of your life, but this game never fails to impress players with the value of visually presenting ideas, thoughts, and feelings.

I. Open your journal to two blank, facing pages. Draw

a triangle that fills each page.

At the apex of one triangle, write "Joyful." At the left bottom corner, write "Enthusiastic," and at the bottom right corner, write "Content." On the opposite triangle, write "Fearful" at the apex, "Jealous" at the left bottom corner, and "Impatient" at the right bottom.

II. Set a timer for three minutes. On the "Fearful" triangle, begin filling in with other words from The Feeling List (page 26).

Place each word on the triangle in the location that feels best. Note that each word will be positioned near other words of similar meaning and feeling. Add some words of your own as they occur to you. When the timer goes off, stop!

III. Immediately begin to work on the "Joyful" triangle.

Set the timer for a full ten minutes and repeat the above steps, this time filling the "Joyful" triangle with words from the upper half of The Feeling List. Don't feel limited if you want to keep going after the timer rings. Notice your mood lighten as you spend time with the words that express a higher-vibration state.

IV. As soon as you've completed work on the "Joyful" triangle, turn to the next page in your journal and write your impressions of this activity.

How did it feel to work within the "Fearful" triangle"? Was it difficult to place the words? Which triangle was easier to fill in? Were you ready to stop when the timer rang?

Write Free

<u>Some tips</u>: This game succeeds best when you recall times in your life when you've experienced the emotions on the triangle. Recalling the source of a feeling gives a clue to where it should go on the triangle: was it grade school, at your last job, or in a difficult relationship? Connecting your hand to the page is a fabulous way to acquire understanding about a feeling: the process harnesses the power of your combined emotional, motor, and intellectual skills. The result is remarkable!

✍ Positive Depths

Yes, the positive has depths, too. And there's no better way to explore just how positive you can be than to go deep into your writing. Writing as a means of self-exploration is a fabulous tool. It doesn't require that you know where you're going or even the genre, length, or tone of your piece of writing. It simply requires that you plumb the depths of your feelings about a subject. Allowing yourself time to write about a subject, from the core of your being, means truly exploring—listening to your heart and mind and letting your hand translate.

As a means of plumbing the depths of the positive, the next activity explores words that are associated with happy times in your life.

I. Begin by imagining a person, place, or thing that inspires joy in you. Write it down.

Example: *I love the Green River in Utah.*

II. Now, remember four images associated with the statement in Step 1. Write them down.

Example: 1.   *thunderstorms*

2. *sagebrush*

3. *playful waves*

4. *summer heat*

Pick the four images that occur to you first; they're likely to be the strongest. If another vies for your attention as well, add it to the list or replace one of the other images. This is your chance to recall sights, sounds, smells, anything sensory, about a person, place, or thing. Do you remember the rooster calling from across the river? The smell of morning coffee from the camp stove? How about the way your friend smiled when she saw you returning from a long hike? The four images should express these sensations in a few words.

III. Next, set a timer for ten minutes. In your journal, write "Positive Plumbing, Scene 1" at the top of a blank page. Then freewrite, without stopping and without censoring, until you've incorporated all four images on your list.

> Example: *I love the Green River in Utah in the summertime. In the heat of the afternoon, there's a thunderstorm almost every day. When the rain falls, even just a little, it wets the sage and releases that fabulous spicy scent. It makes me feel alive to...*

Take your time. Don't feel in a hurry to include all the images. Just have the list in front of you with the assignment to work them all in. You'll get to each one in good time. If the timer goes off and you've missed one or two, keep going. Set the timer again if it'll help. Continue for as long as you care to, but go for at least the first ten minutes even if you get all images in the first sentence and it only takes you ten seconds. Stay with the images that build the positive scene: the neighbor who raised horses, the color of the river in the afternoon, the sound of the cattle guard when a truck rattled over it, the rain that settled the dust. Mine your imagination. Plumb the depths of that positive place and time. You'll be amazed how great it feels to use your pen and your imagination to rebuild a scene you love on paper.

Some tips: This game can be played with neutral or negative images, too, if your goal is to write other scenes besides the positive. For the purpose of creating settings in which you feel your power, though, and in which your main character (yourself) can move around with ease and grace, going deep into the images you love serves to transport you to a wonderful world that can be accessed at any time.

PART TWO

REVISING

Actively revising the life you want to live

Part One guided you through clearing out the clutter of your negative feelings the way you might clear off your desk before beginning a new project. As writers and creative souls, you know the power and purpose of a blank page (and its many artistic corollaries). Blank does not connote empty, but clear and quiet, a space of stillness and calm from which you will now begin to create pictures, images, ideas, and intentions that will lead to your desires.

Perhaps the most important point you can carry with you through Part Two is this: to get what you want, you must know what you want. It is so simple a concept, it's often the easiest to overlook. Our desires are often nebulous, or show up as longing, which is a form of focusing on what you don't have (and thereby creating more of the same). Identifying what you do desire in the Write Free method is as simple as writing it down. Think of it like making a trip to the grocery store. If you go shopping to replenish your pantry for the week, but you go without a list, you are more likely to purchase items on a whim that aren't necessarily what you want to buy. Without a list, you're at the mercy of your appetite and impulses, and could come home with a basket full of snacks but nothing for dinner.

Identifying what you want for your artistic life is the same. If your vision is blurry—maybe all you know is that you want to live in a natural setting, work from home, and live in a quaint cottage—would you be happy in just any natural setting, whether desert or greenery? Would you be happy in any cottage, such as a one-room fixer-upper? Not likely! You have preferences. The more concrete, visual, and detailed your preferences are to you, the more you will connect your desires—that perfect cottage in the peaceful woods with a calming stream singing outside your window—with the positive emotions that come when you are happy!

We call this process of identifying and clarifying your desires revising. In writing, revising is the process of taking your work to a deeper level, of getting clear and strengthening the work. So it is with your life. In the act of revising, your pen or keyboard are much more powerful than the simple instruments you believe they are; an instrument allows you to record your preferences in full, vivid relief and then change them as you want them to. Feelings can be revised too, by shifting from one to another, thus changing the eventual result and attracting your desires into being. To Write Free requires no more complicated technology than a way to become clear about what your desires are, and the willingness to feel good about them. When you revise your desires, your feelings, and your methods for your writing life, you create a new template, erase the old default, and most important, you get to be the one in charge of your revision. No critical editor or judge will tell you what is right; only you will know. In the act of revising, you follow your own formula and refine it until it feels right!

The more detailed you can be in writing, the greater the energy and momentum you will pick up and add to the ultimate creation of your desires. The minute you begin identifying the spectacular, possibly unexamined details of your desires, the nature of attraction promises that they

Write Free

are already coming into being.

We hope that you will revise your old black-and-white desires into full color until they are so real that you can't wait to touch, feel, hold, visit, and live them. Revising puts the power of change in your hands.

At some point in our lives, most of us have felt at the whim of circumstances, the random order of life "happening" to us. Most of us simply ride the current to the best of our abilities. What if we could actually control the current, know when it would be bumpy or smooth? What if, even better, we could ask the current to be exactly as we want it to be? Revising enables you to redo and remake scenarios in your life that did not go as you preferred. You can make everyone say the right things, behave ideally, and see results turn out exactly as you want them to about anything. If you can shift the way you feel about things, you actively create better feelings that will deliver better events, circumstances, and situations to you.

Revising is all about possibilities. It's a surefire method to remind you that at any given moment you are in charge of creating your artistic life, all by the seemingly simple act of writing your way there.

CHAPTER FOUR

Unleashing Your Desires

*Writing gives you a great opportunity
to swim through to freedom.*

—Natalie Goldberg

Jordan writes:

My friend Christie is a New England-based writer who has been writing her whole life. She always considered herself a "positive" person in tune with her feelings, except for one area: she had a steady negative stream of defeating thoughts and beliefs about her writing.

"For years I had been giving in to the negative voices in my head allowing myself to believe that I had no right to be a writer, that no journal should accept my stories, and no agent would ever consider me worthy of representation," she said.

Christie knew what she wanted—to be a successfully published literary writer—but she hadn't yet shifted her feelings about the process.

Tired of the rejections and the frustration she felt, she wrote in her journal that she needed "a change in attitude." Not long after, a friend of hers turned her on to the idea of the power of attraction.

"As I learned to identify my desires and revise them, things started to happen. I paid more and more attention to what I was thinking and feeling and actively working to make myself feel and believe and want otherwise. Every day I wrote new desires in my journal and reread my old ones—continuing to add to them and make them richer. As time passed, things started to happen," she said.

These "things" included having essays and stories published in quick succession by top-tier literary publications she had coveted for years, and then, a surprising request by a literary agent to represent her fiction. Christie's work is now being represented by this agent.

"I firmly believe that taking the time to work with my desires and learn to listen to my feelings helped me attract representation. I am eternally grateful to my friend who showed me the way."

Desires are funny things. They can preoccupy us, or seem to ebb right out of us if we stop giving them our attention. There are some desires that have probably been burning in your unconscious for as long as you can remember; childhood dreams or lifelong aspirations that may have gone unrealized for any number of reasons. And there are minor desires that you know you can live without but that would be nice if they were fulfilled. None of your desires are wrong or better than any other. But the more desires you can draw to mind that make you excited, passionate, inspired, and feeling great when you think about them, the better they will serve you in the activities in this book.

Maybe you haven't really given much thought to what you want lately. Maybe life has gotten away from you, and you've put your wants on a shelf for "later," when there is more of that elusive "free" time and fewer responsibilities. "Later" is a time that never comes, however. The time for identifying your biggest desires is now. Right now! The moment you opened this chapter, you began to pave the way for getting what you want, despite all the other responsibilities and reasons claiming your attention.

In this chapter you will take down those dusty desires from the "later" shelf, shine them up, and remember why it is that you want them. Not only that, but you will learn to turn up the volume on these desires so that you can visualize them in full, vivid detail, and begin to anticipate them being realized.

When you begin to pay attention to the power of attraction, you will notice that what you focus on, you bring into being. You've probably heard the phrase, "like attracts like" before. Attracting your desires works the same way; if you till a space of earth in your backyard for a garden, for instance, you're far more likely to actually plant flowers than if you sit staring at a patch of grass. And once you begin thinking about what to plant in that garden, suddenly you notice a new nursery in town, and discounts for flowers turn up in your mailbox, and friends suddenly have to offload a bunch of rare bulbs. It seems a bit like magic, but once you've focused your attention on your desire, you are more inclined to look for, attract, and take advantage of opportunities to create your goal.

There are an abundance of resources waiting to help bring your desires into being, but first you have to take the step, put rake or hoe in hand, and dig up that patch of earth.

So if your desire is to be a published novelist, but you're holding thoughts about how hard that is, how you're not sure you can write well enough, or if you should stick to your day job as a real estate agent, then you're still sitting and staring at a patch of grass, frustrated that you don't have any flowers.

The activities in this section are designed to help you clarify which desires really raise your passions and to provide effective tools to flower them into being.

ACTIVITIES

✍My Number One Desire

You probably have more desires than you can count on your fingers, so this game may challenge you at first. We want you to pick your Number One desire for your artistic life and write it at the top of a blank page in your Write Free notebook. If a genie popped out of a bottle tomorrow and said you could have ONLY ONE wish granted, this would be that desire. In other words, if two of your desires were one, to write and produce your own play, and two, to clean out the filing cabinet, you'll want to go with the one that excites you most at the mere thought of it, probably the desire to be a playwright.

I. Write your number one desire at the top of a fresh piece of paper now.

II. Spend at least one minute contemplating how great this desire feels.

III. Number from 1 to 25 down the left side of the page.

If you want something enough, you can probably think of some good reasons why you want it, a few "impractical" reasons, and a handful of reasons that seem to matter only to you. That's good, because you're going to have the chance to apply every possible kind of reason to this important desire right now. We suggest that your reasons be written in positive terms, even though your desire is not yet a reality.

IV. Under each of the twenty-five spaces, write one reason why you want what you want. Give yourself a few moments to feel the positive energy of each reason. No reason is too small, or too grand. You can want it because you think it will achieve world peace, or simply because it gives you a flash of pleasure. See if you can let this pleasurable anticipation build as you write, so that by the time you hit twenty-five, you are buzzing with excitement and good feelings.

Example: *I want to write and produce my own play. Why?*

1. *Because it will be creatively fulfilling*

2. *I will get to use talents that I don't otherwise get to use.*

3. *I love the simplicity of the play form*

4. *It will be more fun than weeding...*

<u>Some tips</u>: If you slow down and think you are running out of reasons, don't quit!! Stick with it. Think of the simplest possible reason why you want it. No positive reason is too small! Don't consider what others will think. Allow yourself to want and don't worry about how this will come to you yet.

Congratulate yourself for getting these down! The time spent on visualizing your desires is important. You are setting the groundwork for your creative life.

✍ But Why?

You know how children, in their perfect innocence, are often unsatisfied with the simplest of answers? "Mom, why do birds fly?" And Mom answers, "Because they have wings." And the child asks again, "But why do they have wings?" and so on... You're going to apply that same kind of innocent, childlike curiosity to this next game.

I. From your list of twenty-five wonderful reasons why you want your Number One Desire, pull five that resonate with you most. They can draw you the strongest for any reason. Write them on a fresh page.

II. Take each reason, and ask in a spirit of curiosity and anticipation, WHY will [your desire here] make me feel creatively fulfilled? And so on. For each of these five reasons, ask WHY again, and freewrite the answers. You may come up with a whole series of new answers to the question, or deeper, possibly surprising reasons that didn't make it onto your list of twenty-five. If you are feeling particularly keen to push your feeling state up even higher, do this activity for as many of your twenty-five reasons as you like.

✍ Telling a Story

Even if your medium is poetry (or sculpture, for that matter), the act of telling a story is a powerful incantation that can draw your desires to you. Remember stories told to you by adults when you were a child? Remember how those characters were as real to you as your actual friends? Your desires are only intangible so long as you can't see or know them. Now that you know why you want them, it's time to tell yourself a new story, one that you'll begin to live by, reshaping and refining it until it vividly becomes the story you want your life to be.

On your Number One Desire list you have twenty-five reasons why you want something. From the But Why game, you have plumbed the depths of your desire, and can see that desires are a meaningful, intrinsic part of who you are. In this next game, you are going to employ all your senses to write a narrative story, making your way to the end result: HAVING your Number One Desire. As you follow the guided writing below, include specific details of how things feel, smell, look, taste, and sound. Be sure to remember that everything in your story is there to lead you toward what you want. Every character that shows up, all objects and ideas you encounter should line up to support your desire. If a blip of the negative finds its way in, start a new sentence with the intention of moving away from any negativity. This game challenges you to use your imagination, which happens to be one of the most powerful tools at your disposal for creating what you want.

I. Begin by imagining yourself in a dark room in which you can't see anything, but where you feel perfectly safe and brimming with anticipation. A seam of light appears, revealing a door opening. As you step through that door, you are going to storytell your way to the fulfillment of your desire. Begin writing with the sentence: "As the door opens, I am brimming with anticipation..." By the end of your writing, your goal is to have reached your desire, and see it as vividly as possible. It will seem real to you.

Some tips: Focusing your attention on what you want instantly begins to draw it to you. If you can feel as though you already have what you want, you begin to embody it, and thus create it through your actions and feelings. Never underestimate the power of your imagination. If you can envision having the creative life you dream of, and continue to drum up more energy around having it, you will be pleasantly surprised by the outcome. Don't take our word for it. Try it.

CHAPTER FIVE

If You Know It, You Can Change It

*Knowledge is happiness, because to have knowledge—
broad, deep knowledge—is to know true ends from false
and lofty things from low.*

—Helen Keller

Jordan writes:

It's easy to let the demon of negativity tug you into its chambers. This is why we recommend practicing writing daily, even if you don't feel "skilled" or like an "expert." Simple shifts can make huge changes.

I wrote short stories for a long time before it became clear to me that my true joy and reward was in novel writing. From time to time I still pull out a story, dust it off, polish it up, and usually submit it with the most blasé of attitudes. I must apply extra awareness to my feelings or else the leaden heaviness of doubt will sink me.

Recently I sent a story to a publication that had accepted other stories of mine, so I knew they liked my style. As I sent the manuscript off, I had a feeling of powerful certainty that they would accept it. Many of my successes have sprung from this feeling, so I knew I was doing something right.

Sure enough, they responded with a note saying, "We really like this but we need to hold onto it for a few more days to decide. Do you mind?" Of course I didn't mind! What were a few extra days for success?

I went about my business feeling extremely good—as acceptance or its potential tend to make me feel.

Then I let in a niggling worm of doubt. What if they want me to change something? What if it isn't good enough? Sure enough, I got an e-mail back from the editor the next day saying, "We really think it needs to be in first person point of view. Are you willing to change it? If so, there's still no guarantee that we'll take it, but we'd love to see it that way."

Already in a disappointed state, I went ahead and made the change—it did make it a stronger story—and resubmitted it. Only now the voice in my mind was saying, "Oh, they'll never take it."

And they didn't. They even gave me explicit reasons why not.

I was about to let myself wallow in the soul-sucking state of rejection when this thought came to my mind: "How can you turn this around and create a positive outcome? How can you shift this feeling, because if you don't, you know where it's going to take you." Indeed, I could see the burbling cauldron of defeat and I didn't want to dip so much as a hair in it.

I reread the rejection, because it had sparked an idea in me, an idea that I'd wanted to write about for months. I began to scratch out the rough idea for an essay. At the end of an hour, I was not only over my feeling of rejection but I had also transformed it into the triumph of writing something I liked.

That's not the end, either! The next day, when I spoke

Write Free

with my editor for a national writing magazine that I regularly contribute to, she told me that they were restructuring and accepting fewer of the "how-to" articles I had been writing; instead, they were looking for essays. Essays! Like the one I had just written! I pitched my idea, which she liked, sent her a draft of the essay that had been born out of my 'rejection,' and it was accepted for publication. That is the power of paying attention to your feelings.

✿

"Knowledge is half the battle" is the common cry of self-help literature. Whether or not knowledge is half the battle—and who wants their creative life to be a battle anyway—knowledge and action do create an important balance. Acting on your desires without knowledge is blind grasping; knowing what you want without doing anything about it is stalling your dreams. Chapter Five is designed to bring out in the open the tricks we use to keep ourselves from our desires, and offer easy, whimsical methods to get back on track.

On the path to knowing what you want, it's important to get a good look at the critical voices that tumble out in a chorus each time you put forth what you do want. You likely know these voices all too well; they may even mimic the voices of real people you know who are ruled by their fears. You can't do that. How will you make a living? What if it doesn't succeed?

The first four chapters have helped you carve a path through the highs and lows of your feelings, have given you practice in focusing on what you want and how to feel good about those desires. The activities have given you a crucial amount of knowledge, more than enough to begin spending at least one minute each day focused on feeling good about what you want. To generate even more positive feeling energy for what you want, we will dally temporarily in the dark water of some common sabotage techniques, just long enough to see them for what they are and banish them.

ACTIVITIES

✍ A Case of the "Yeah, Buts"

Underneath all of your greatest desires are little gremlins known as the "yeah, buts..." These are the voices that pop into your head after you have expressed your desire. They say terrible things like, "yeah, but if you do that, your mother will never speak to you again." Or, "yeah, but who do you think you are?" The "yeah, buts" have the effect of cutting off open, positive feeling and inviting in vibrations of lack and negativity. Our goal is to guide you to keeping open to the positive joy of your desires.

I. Write five "yeah, buts" that come to mind when you look at your number one desire from Chapter Four (or any desire that is pressing at you right now).

Example: *I want to have a career as a successful novelist.*

1. *Yeah, but nobody can actually make a living that way.*

2. *Yeah, but how will I get started?*

3. *Yeah, but you need lots of time to write novels, which I don't have.*

4. *Yeah, but what will my family think?*

5. *Yeah, but I'll never be good enough.*

Take a moment to notice how your body feels, how your heart feels. What sorts of thoughts have come to your mind? Write these in your notebook now as you read over your "yeah, buts."

✐ Transforming

There is a surprisingly small difference between actually having what you want, and feeling as though you have what you want. You know that state of being that arises right before something happens that you're looking forward to? Like a night out, a birthday gift, or a rejuvenating weekend? That heightened state of anticipation can be had at any moment. Treat everything you want as if they're already on their way to you, and you'll add power to your ability to attract them. If you can effectively feel the joy and wonder of having what you want before you have it, you will create it.

I. Take the most convincing "yeah, but" from above, the one that really hooks its spiny little fingers into you, and write it at the top of a blank page.

Example: *Yeah, I want to be a published novelist, but my writing just isn't good enough.*

Next, you're going to drain the power source of this negative voice and turn it into a statement of joy that you can feel. Using your personal example, write a dialogue between the voice of the "yeah, but" and a higher part of yourself, a "guide" whose only job is to remind you how perfectly appropriate and wonderful it is to want this, and to defend you against your irritating little "yeah, buts." Here's an example of how it works:

Yeah, I want to be published, but my writing just isn't good enough.

Inner Wisdom/Guide:

Well, whose silly standard is that?

Reply:

> *Yeah, I don't know, but it's just the way it
> will always be.*

Inner Wisdom/Guide:

> *You always speak in negatives. What if you
> just wrote the novel and worried about
> judging it later?*

The goal is to take a good look at how weak these "yeah, buts" become once you apply reason, joy, and imagination to them. "Yeah, buts" are echoes of fear, of other people's beliefs, of standards that you did NOT set for yourself, but have been following out of pressure, fear, or obligation. They generally do nothing but sabotage you.

Once you have written sufficient dialogue to take you where you can effectively hear that "yeah, but" and not be intimidated by it, do another one. Do as many as you need to do, and finish the game with this final, joy-enhancing exercise:

II. Write whichever "yeah, but" you're working on one final time on a new page. It's best to write it in pencil, to show how ephemeral and erasable it is. Then write below it:

The reasons I no longer believe this "yeah, but" are:
> (for example)

> *It's more important to just show up and write.*

> *I am committed to improving myself, and
> am a dedicated reviser.*

> *Only a very uncreative person would give in
> to that negative voice.*

I have proved to myself that I can write,
and write well.

Some tips: For each affirmation you write to counteract the negative voice of the "yeah, but" allow yourself to FEEL the powerful emotions of the positive. Feel proud, certain, successful, determined, joyful, creative, and persistent. Let those feelings build one upon the other until you are buzzing with good energy.

✍ What If?

Being human means that our "best" not only varies from day to day, but can also be hard to rally. Let's face it, some days our "higher" selves are taking an extended nap, or need two more cups of coffee before they show up. Maybe you received an unpleasant letter, or felt your creative energy was blocked. Maybe you felt daunted by the sheer number of ideas you have for projects you'd like to start. Well don't worry, there's an activity for days like these:

I. Imagination is a powerfully attractive force. When you imagine something you want to have, you may think you are only dreaming fancifully, but you are actually creating space for your desires to come into being. The more you imagine what you want, the more energy you create around your desire, the more you are drawing it to you. So on those days when imagining is the most you can muster, you're doing a lot more than you think. Allow yourself to imagine/daydream on the page anything at all that you want, from the most extraordinary to the most mundane. Don't give yourself a goal, just write until you're done.

Example:

1. *What if I got a book deal like J. K.Rowling and could buy a Victorian mansion?*

2. *What if I painted my office; I wonder if it would make me feel more inspired?*

3. *What if the neighbor's dog just stopped barking for the two hours I need to write?*

4. *What if I met an editor by chance on an airplane who took my manuscript?*

5. *What if I could just write a poem a day?*

Some tips: During this activity, allow your mind to let loose. Don't FORCE desires on yourself, just let things flow in. Put on some music; open the windows if you can. Do this activity in the most restful, relaxed, even whimsical mood possible. This activity is not at all about doing, but about allowing yourself to muse and fantasize, play, and wonder without the pressure of wondering HOW it will come to pass.

✍ And So It Is!

Now that you've allowed yourself to play and muse without the pressure of having to do anything about it, you're going to take this "what if" scenario one step further by imagining that each of the things on your list has ALREADY come to pass.

I. For each "what if" you are going to write a line or two about how it FELT (yes, that's past tense, pretending it already has happened) when your "what if" came to pass.

The circumstances may be dreamed up, but trust us, the feelings won't be false. Even though none of these things may have happened yet, you can tap into how you imagine you will feel (and for this purpose, already feel), when you got what you mused about having. At the end of each statement of feelings we urge you to add the slogan: "And so it is!"

Example:

1. *What if I got a book deal like J. K. Rowling and could buy a Victorian Mansion? I will never forget how grateful I felt the day I signed the final papers and picked up the key to my new house. I stood staring at it like I was in a Merchant-Ivory film, and real tears of gratitude flowed to my eyes. I had made this happen! And so it is!*

2. *What if I painted my office; I wonder if it would make me feel more inspired? I was amazed what a little paint could do! Before the smell of paint was out of the room I suddenly had the urge to clean off my desk, and then my closet, and before I knew it I had a whole new office and with it, a bubbling flow of new ideas. That simple change opened up a font of energy in my writing. I felt so inspired! And so it is!*

3. *What if the neighbor's dog just stopped barking for the two hours I need to write? When the first day passed and Tilly didn't make a peep from 2 to 4, I cried with relief. The next day, I rushed excitedly to my notebook to get down everything that was flowing to me. Pretty soon I stopped noticing if she was even barking at all because my writer's block had passed! And so it is!*

Write Free

<u>Some tips</u>: When you are attracting your desires, the only tools you need are your good feelings and the ability to know what it is you want. So why not feel good about things you want before they happen? It only works in your favor!

Living Your Story

Each life is an encyclopedia, a library, an inventory
of objects ... and everything can be constantly shuffled
and reordered in every way conceivable.

—Italo Calvino

Jordan writes:

I am a novelist at heart, and the plaintive cry of my creative self has grown louder and more powerful over the years; it reached a crescendo when I worked at my last "day" job for a lovely nonprofit environmental organization. I had been freelance writing for local publications on the side for years. But what I really wanted was a life where I worked from home, could set my own schedule, and decide exactly when and how to write the novels I have inside. I always felt a sense of longing and soon realized that I was more often focused on what I didn't have; my attention was stuck in "lack." Using The Wish List (Chapter Ten) and other activities in this book, I envisioned what it would be like to have my dream life, how it would feel to wake up each morning with only my own goals to pursue, and to have the satisfaction of holding my first published novel in my hand.

Without seeking them out, job offers started to appear by way of friends. Magazine editing jobs, reporting jobs, copyediting jobs. None of these was perfect, but I took serious note of their sudden appearance as proof that the attractive force of my Write Free play was working. After all, these were jobs having to do with writing! I imagined myself in each job, pictured how far I would have to commute, and what the benefits would be versus the cost to my creative writing. I let myself feel how each job would affect and change my life if I took it. None seemed right, so I held out, intrigued by what else I could attract through wanting and envisioning. Each morning and night I wrote more vivid descriptions of the writing life I wanted, adding new and more precise elements to it because I believed that these other jobs were signs that if I got really clear about what I wanted, and felt really good about having it, it would come to me.

Two months later, my husband came to me after I'd had a particularly difficult day working to achieve the goals of others. He said, "It's time. You need to quit and work from home. I can feel it." He trusted my self-discipline and was tired of seeing me unhappy. With his support, I made the leap, telling myself I would not allow myself to be afraid, that fear was only a distraction that would keep away my desires. Within two weeks, two new freelance sources appeared to me, again without solicitation on my part, from seeds planted awhile back, one from years before! These two gigs provided me with almost exactly the same income I had made at my day job, and over time that income has increased. Today my latest novel is being represented by a respected literary agent.

☼

As a creative person, you are likely aware of how creative energy is both in your control and yet seems to be channeled through you by something else. How many times have you sat down to write or create something and been surprised by what follows? This element of surprise is part of the joy of creating. If you don't make the time to sit down with your notebook, or canvas or other medium, the muses will have a difficult time getting through the doors.

Many creative people who have day jobs discover that they must rise early, a few hours before their actual job begins, to carve out just a whisper of time in their busy schedules to write or be creative. Parents often learn how to practice their art inside the tiny windows of children's nap times. You may find at first that making time for writing and creating feels difficult or like "extra" work on top of all that you already must do in your life. But armed with the awareness of the power of attraction, and by doing the Write Free work, what you may not realize is that by giving yourself that extra hour, or even fifteen minutes every day, you are chiseling out the space for more creative time.

Each bit of space you carve out for your creative life widens the possibilities, like a tunnel being dug with a spoon, though it may seem to happen almost imperceptibly. To attract your good is far simpler than you may realize. All you need to do is focus your attention (and intention) for one minute a day on your desires in a state of feel-good anticipation, and every day this tunnel into your creative life grows larger, spoonful by spoonful, page by page, moment by moment.

Chapter Six is designed to remind you that just a little effort is required every day toward the goal of your creative life. Actually, the word "effort" is misleading; what is required of you each day is more equivalent to attention.

If you can train yourself to rise with a feeling that THIS DAY will be the day you hear the news you want—that your loan came through so you can buy that lovely cottage, that your story has been accepted for publication in a coveted journal, that your request to take Fridays off work has been approved—then you are "working" the power of attraction. Your desires are already taking shape, whether you can see them or not.

ACTIVITIES

✍ Making a Plan

By now you've spent a lot of time getting to know what you want. Your ideas are beginning to crystallize; be proud of all that you've done so far! Maybe you've cleaned out your filing cabinet for the first time in ten years; perhaps you told your family that for one hour every day you will only be available to yourself, to write. Even if you have not yet made any decisions of this nature, you've surely begun to think of what you'd like to change. Those thoughts are crucial to this next game.

I. Select something you would like to do, but have not yet done, specifically to nurture, expand, or allow your creative life to flower open as you have imagined. Let's call this "making a plan." Write this plan in your Write Free notebook.

Examples:

1. *I plan to cloister myself in the den from 3 to 4 p.m. every day to write in my notebook.*

2. *I plan to ask my boss for Fridays off.*

3. *I plan to pull out all my old short stories and organize them in a folder so I know where to start in revising them.*

II. Good! Now imagine that today is the first day that you are doing whatever you planned to do: cloistering yourself in the den for the first time, or standing in your boss's office about to ask him for Fridays off. Describe to yourself, in writing, what you expect to experience when putting your intention into action. Focus on your feelings. Allow the possibilities to flow through you.

Picture yourself in the den, writing in the afternoon as envisioned. What do you expect the house will sound like at this time of day? Are the roads being improved with jackhammers on your block? Or can you hear the sweet trill of birds outside your window?

Next picture yourself requesting Fridays off at work. You're in the boss's office, notebook in hand. Is your boss's office a place you always dread? Do you imagine him to be happy to see you, or concerned? Write it out in complete and HONEST detail. What do you really expect to happen?

Remember in Chapter Five we told you that there is a surprisingly small difference between feeling as though you have something and actually having it? The same thing goes for expectations. If you picture things going badly, you are pulling negativity toward you by expecting it.

III. Now, read over the expectations you have just written. Maybe you expect your boss to laugh and say, "Are you crazy?" Maybe you expect that you will not be confident enough to make a strong case for how you plan to make it work. Or perhaps you expect that you will be too distracted by the dust in your den to concentrate on writing.

Now you're going to take this game a step further, by expecting the intention to go exactly as you would like it to go. First, take your same intention from above, but this time add the phrase, "I expect it will go exactly as I desire." Write this at the top of a blank page.

Write Free

Example: *I plan to ask my boss for Fridays off,
and I expect it will go exactly as I desire.*

IV. Now write out your plan exactly as you would like
it to happen in exquisite detail. Write in the present tense,
beginning with yourself waking up on the day that you will
set your intention in motion.

Example:

> *I wake to a cloudless morning, with a soft pink
> light flooding my room. I haven't even gotten
> out of bed before I am filled with a feeling of
> blissful anticipation. The sound of the birds out-
> side my window seems like a message to me that
> whatever I want today, I can have. I take delight
> in each sip of my coffee and its strong, rich
> aroma. My drive to work feels easy and slow. I
> am aware of my breath, and the traffic doesn't
> bother me. Next Friday I will not be making this
> drive; I will be in my office, writing. Today is the
> day I will ask for what I need and will get it.*

> *When I arrive at work, I spot my boss in the
> lounge drinking his coffee. I don't feel my cus-
> tomary twinge of anxiety upon seeing him. He
> is really a very nice man, just overworked, just
> another human being making a living...*

> *Approaching his office, I notice the vines growing
> outside his window have sprouted red, trumpet-
> shaped flowers, and this gives me a feeling of
> hope. I knock on his door and he greets me with
> a smile. "Isn't this a beautiful morning?" he says,
> and seems to be in an unusually good mood... I
> can tell he will be receptive to anything I ask.*

<u>Some tips</u>: Don't worry if some embellishments on the truth wind up in this game. Maybe there aren't really any trumpet-shaped flowers outside of your boss's window, but the fact that they have shown up in your writing is a sign of hope; the hand of your own creative impulse adds elements that make you feel good about the scene. Things that heighten feelings of hopefulness, calm, and even excitement are worth adding. Don't veer too far off from the possible (stay on planet Earth), however, because you want to put this scenario into play in real life.

What you're doing is retraining your expectations by writing them down. You learned how to storytell in Chapter Five; now you are finding out the practical purpose of storytelling. For every desire you have, you can create new expectations for how you would like this desire to come to you, thus attracting its essence.

✍ Shaping the Day

Now that you've learned how to retrain your expectations, we want you to apply this art of scripting to each day of your life.

Morning is the most potent part of your day. It sets in motion the rest of the day, which establishes the direction for the next day, and so on ad infinitum. If you wake in a state of anxiety, you're already carrying a load of negative energy that can act like a vortex, pulling you away from all that you intend and want for that day.

I. Choose to "shape the day" in one of two ways:

What do you want tomorrow to feel and look like?

What do you want today to feel and look like?

Choose one of the two ways to write about shaping your day. If you choose to write about Friday the day before, for example, you will give yourself a little bit more time in advance to build up a vortex of good-feeling energy, investing in Friday's fabulousness on Thursday. If you choose to write about Friday ON Friday, do so in the morning, as close to the first thing as you can allow.

Example:

Today/Tomorrow Friday the 22nd of July, my day will unfold as follows: I will rise when my alarm goes off and therefore will be able to dress and get ready slowly and luxuriously. I will drink herbal tea as part of my goal to be gentler on my body and be sure to eat breakfast so that by lunch I will not be light-headed. I will take deep breaths all day and focus on whatever activity I am doing, not rushing, not getting ahead of myself. Because I will be going slowly and consciously, everything that I do will be done easily and with a sense of fun. Phone calls I've been waiting for will come today. My co-worker will have nice things to say to me, and I will feel more patient and friendly with my staff than usual. As a result, I will actually finish my work for the day ahead of the game, and will be able to leave an hour early so I can stop by that lovely new café and spend an hour writing before I go home to make dinner.

Some tips: The further in advance of your day you do this, the more time you'll have to build the feeling of how wonderful that slow, easy day is going to be. Do these activities every day, or as often as you can, and you will start to notice changes. At first these may seem like "coincidences," until you recognize your own hand in the creation of them.

✍ The First Day of Your Life

Have you ever heard the axiom, "Today is the first day of the rest of your life?" Ever thought about what that means, corny as it may sound? In this final activity, you'll have an opportunity to tap the power of that simplistic saying; you'll get to write about the first day of the rest of your life, thereby creating it.

I. Imagine waking up on the first day after all the desires for your writing life have been fulfilled.

Your original set of goals for your creative life are complete, and now you are making new goals for things you didn't even think were possible. This "new" you is going to write a letter to someone you haven't seen since all these changes happened and knows nothing about them.

II. Communicate to this person the following information: What your life is like, and more importantly what it feels like NOW.

Example:

> *Dear long-lost friend. I have so much to tell you, so sit tight as this will be a very long letter...*

Your task is to imagine what changes have happened, and how they have affected you, those you love, and your future. Have your life changes had a ripple effect? Did your published book change the lives of others? Did your appearance on national television set a new trend into motion?

The fulfilled you is looking back on your life, remembering your concerns, fears, and beliefs that existed before you began this work, though you no longer feel attached to them. You are delighted by the shifts and fulfillment you've experienced, and you're communicating this in letter form to someone who has not been around to see it firsthand.

Some tips: This activity requires you to suspend all disbelief and enter into a state of heightened imagination. Don't skimp on details. This is the new you, the new life. Tell your friend everything!

PART THREE

FEELING YOUR STORY

Focusing on positive feelings to create your desires

By now you're familiar with the idea that attracting the creative life you desire (and deserve) is determined by how you feel about it. Even so, we're all human, subject to moods that peak, dip, and twist, depending on life's circumstances.

In Part One you learned that feeling better is the first step to feeling good. We encourage you to come back to these activities when feeling good is a challenge. In Part Two you learned to take an active role—preparing, envisioning, and imagining your way to feeling good.

Here, in Part Three, we want to strengthen the foundation you've begun to build. We want to remind you that our feelings are with us all the time, and these feelings, no matter how tiny or fleeting, add up to the cumulative experience of your life. If you can do the activities in this book in the spirit of fun and creative exploration, you will enhance the process that is already working.

The activities in Part Three will also help you to identify changes in your life that are the result of your work with the power of attraction. Noticing the results is an important part of the process and helps you keep at it. The more you keep at it, the more your life and your writing will take on the precise shape you want. Part Three will train you to look for signs that attractive energy is working in your life, in all directions. Rejoice and delight in getting what you want, and hold out for your dreams to materialize exactly as you want them.

CHAPTER SEVEN

Feelings Create Our Reality

*The greatest happiness is to transform
one's feelings into action.*

—Madame de Stael

Jordan writes:

My friend Philip Beard is the acclaimed author of two published novels, *Dear Zoe* and *Lost in the Garden*. Philip's road to publication was very unusual, or as he puts it: "The story of how *Dear Zoe* found its way to Viking is one I still have trouble believing. If you have ever doubted the combined powers of blind persistence and serendipity, then listen to the rest of my story."

After practicing law full time for eleven years, Philip began writing his first novel, billing just enough law hours from home to make family grocery money. He finished his novel in nine months, and a year later secured a wonderful agent to represent it. Six months later, his agent received the last of the twenty-seven rejection letters, and *The Love Number* went back in the drawer. Fortunately, he had followed his agent's advice and was already halfway through a first draft of a second novel, and by January 2003, *Dear Zoe* was ready for submission.

Says Philip, "After the first six rejection letters arrived, I was advised by more than one person that I should change the point of view before submitting to any more publishers—that the format of *Dear Zoe* took away from the intimacy between narrator and reader and should be rethought."

Philip was not happy with this advice. It didn't feel right to him. But he was willing to do just about anything to avoid the same fate of rejection for the second book: "I spent a month revising the novel to standard first person, changed the title to "*Z*," then sat and cried when I sent it off that way."

Not surprisingly, the change didn't help. Three months later, the last of the twenty-eight rejection letters arrived.

"I felt lost, directionless, paralyzed by the first real failure of my life," says Philip. "I couldn't picture myself going back to the practice of law full time, yet three attempts to start a new novel went nowhere. My family of chronic overachievers didn't say anything, but I knew they were watching me closely. Then I saw an article in the New York Times about self-publishing and decided to take back control of my new career."

This is the crucial moment in Philip's story. He made a choice that *Dear Zoe* would be published no matter what: "I spent the next six months treating the publication of *Dear Zoe* as my full-time job."

Philip went back to the earlier version of the manuscript—restoring both the original title and the original point of view—and read every text on self-publishing he could find. He formed his own publishing outfit and solicited printers. He found a cover designer, a national distributor willing to take a chance, a tireless, imaginative publicist, and sent the manuscript to every published writer he had ever met asking them to read *Dear Zoe* and consider providing a blurb for the back cover.

The key to finding all of these crucial contributors was, quite simply, not being afraid to ask. Phillip knew his chances of success were minuscule, but he was energized by the ability to control every aspect of the process, by creating and following every small lead.

His story gets more amazing. Just after deciding to self-publish, he was in his favorite independent bookstore, to tell his friend, John, the owner, about his self-publishing plans. John suggested that Philip drop off his book for the Penguin representative who would be coming by later that week. Philip did so.

"A few months later, John called to tell me that the Penguin rep loved *Dear Zoe* and wanted permission to send it to Viking," says Philip. "I told him, 'Of course,' then forgot about it."

On March 23, 2004, on the eve of writing "the largest check of my life to print books I couldn't be sure anyone beyond my Christmas card list would buy," says Philip, he received a very important e-mail from the Penguin representative: "The President of Viking Books called and would like you to call her back."

"It just didn't seem possible that, after four years, a novel of mine was going to find a home in New York on the same day I was finalizing plans to print it myself. Of course, that's exactly what happened."

"Three weeks later," he says, "*Dear Zoe* appeared in the 'Hot Deals' column of Publishers Weekly. Unbelievable."

✪

We've said it once, but we're going to say it again and again: what you feel shapes the experiences you have, the results of your endeavors, and the quality of your life.

In this chapter we seek to remind you that you feel constantly, from little tiny blips of irritation or pleasure as you buy groceries, to big, overpowering feelings that stop you mid-sentence with someone you love. Feelings are the matrix out of which everything material springs.

Do you notice how you feel when you open your front door to leave for work and spot early patches of wildflowers that have bloomed unexpectedly? Do you notice how you feel when you step in melted gum accidentally? How about when you rise each morning or watch the evening news?

None of us notices every single moment, and we're not suggesting you start becoming quite that vigilant. But the more moments you notice, the more you can turn the dial of negative feelings backward, or rev up the engine of good feelings, and the more you will create an immensely positive space for your desires.

ACTIVITIES

✎ I Spy

Do this activity at the end of a day, or use the prior day's experiences if you must do it in the morning. The goal is to slow down and take stock of those things you do not normally notice consciously.

I. Write the first ten events of this day or the prior day that come to mind. They need not be big or memorable, just whatever falls into your mind.

Example:

Watered neighbor's garden; argued with bank teller; read a chapter of library book; called my cousin to congratulate on new baby; sang to myself in shower; bought stamps; had ice cream.

II. Take each "event" one at a time and write how you felt as you had the encounter. Then freewrite. Did the event make you think of anything else? Did it remind you of other events/experiences/memories or feelings? What were you thinking while it happened, or just before or after? Do this with each of your ten events.

Example:

Watered neighbor's garden:

I realized that the wonderful smell I always thought was incense was actually coming from beautiful rose bushes I'd never stopped to look at or smell. Then I realized they had grown into an entire backyard paradise. I wanted to pull out my journal and sit down and write because it was so calm, and this got me thinking: what if I created a similar kind of garden haven for myself? I bet it would encourage me to write more and get out of the house on weekends a lot more.

Argued with bank teller:

I was feeling frustrated at having to pay yet another fee, especially because I'd overspent on an outfit I didn't really need, and it was another event in a string of events that seemed to not be going my way this week. When I look back on it, I started out the week in a really bad mood all because I made the mistake of answering the phone on Monday when my sister-in-law called and I knew I wasn't ready to talk to her...

Be honest with yourself. Did you have judgmental thoughts about your diet or body as you ate ice cream? Or did you just give yourself over to the delight of sugar and milk on your palate? Was it a surprisingly good feeling to spend time in your neighbor's exquisite garden, doing a favor for such kind people? Did you learn something by arguing with the bank teller? Perhaps you've been snapping easily at people lately. Give no less than THREE minutes to each number, and let yourself write and write.

III. Look at your answers. Now, on a fresh piece of paper, answer the following questions: Am I surprised by anything I thought or felt before or after an event? Would I do these same events the same way again? If not, what would I do differently? Did my feelings or thoughts seem to cause or reflect what happened at each incident?

So often we go through the motions of our day unaware that we were just thinking something negative, and then surprised when we have a minor fender bender, or snap at the bank teller, or stub a toe. Similarly, sometimes we fail to notice that the half hour spent watering a neighbor's beautiful garden or hanging out with a beloved person makes us feel better, and that feeling goes with us to work, plays into our interactions with family, and even enters into our creative life. These tiny feelings are like the dots that make up the famous impressionist Georges Seurat's beautiful oil paintings. At a distance, a scene looks as if completely rendered in strokes, but upon inspection, the entire painting depicts a series of appropriately placed dots of color. Our feelings are like these dots of color, and the more of them we have the more the picture of our life emerges from within them.

✍ Fault Lines

I. Write down five recent events that have happened to you that you ascribe as being "negative." This will be especially powerful if they relate to your writing life.

Example:

1. *I forgot to send in a submission by the con test deadline.*

2. *I need a filling for a recently discovered cavity.*

3. *I was given a project that should have been my co-worker's and I got it wrong.*

4. *I didn't get any writing done this week because I watched TV instead.*

5. *I worked too late and didn't leave myself time to read that great book.*

II. Under each event write the answer to the question: Why did this happen to me? Who or what is at fault for this not going as I wanted? BE HONEST about what you really think.

Example:

> *I forgot to send in a submission by the contest deadline: I was overwhelmed with extra work that I had to take on to pay my bills!*

> *I need a filling for a recently discovered cavity: If only my husband didn't have a sweet tooth, I'd exercise better willpower.*

> *I was given a project that should have been my co-worker's and I got it wrong: My co-worker is too pushy and I can't say no.*

When looking over your answers, notice where you point the finger. Are you beating yourself up for circumstances out of your control? Are you making yourself a victim of other's actions? Are you convinced that bad things "just happen" to you? Do you let someone else take the blame for your actions? Finding fault really is like creating a small earthquake in your life. It stirs up a torrent of negativity, makes you and others feel bad, ashamed, unmotivated, sapping you of good, strong creative energy.

III. Now, take those same five things that went wrong and view each one with a compassionate eye. See if you can write your way to a better understanding of why it happened, with the sense that you did your best.

Example:

> *I didn't get any writing done this week because I*

watched TV instead: I was tuning out because I was tired from a week of not saying no to projects at work that I should have said no to. I always watch TV as an escape. I guess if I set better boundaries at work, I'll be less inclined to watch TV, and then have more time to write.

✍ I Feel, Therefore I Am

Ever notice how when something happens that you consider "bad," it can lead to another and another until your whole day is one big string of discontent? Or the opposite happens: someone compliments your hair, you charm your way out of a parking ticket, you find a five-dollar bill on the ground, and a string of positive events is kicked into gear? Think these events are coincidence? Not if you're wearing your attraction glasses, they're not!

I. Below is a list of situations that people find themselves in. After each one, in your notebook write what you expect the likely outcome of each scenario will be based on the feeling state of the described person.

1. Alice was rear-ended and now every time she gets in a car, she scans her rearview mirror for the next likely offender.

2. Ginny is reading library copies of great classic literature because she can't afford a writing program but wants to learn better how to write a book.

3. Brenda is saving up to buy a house. She reads the paper daily, lamenting how the prices keep skyrocketing.

4. Callie wants to write a novel, and so buys advice books that tell her how hard it is to get published.

5. Ferdinand is saving all his extra pocket change and

money for a dream trip he's always wanted to take, though his friends think it's foolish.

6. Dreyfus has a friend who works for a literary agency but he's afraid to offend him by asking if he'll take a look at his short story collection.

7. Eric hates his job and is convinced that because he does not have a college degree, he is stuck there.

8. Harriet spends an industrious weekend cleaning out all the drawers and closets in the room she's always intended to be her writing office even though she doesn't have a desk or a computer yet.

<u>Some tips</u>: Don't be fooled by the simplistic nature of this exercise. What should be obvious to us often is not, and because it's not, we allow negative habits to run us.

II. Now, you're going to do this for yourself. Think of anything you want for your writing life, even your Number One Desire, which you identified in Chapter Four. Now list between five and ten attitudes or fears (we call them "holdbacks") that you have about this desire:

Example: *I want to turn that funky old guest*
            room into my writing office.

Holdbacks:

   My spouse will never allow it.

   It's selfish.

   How will an office make me a successful writer?

   It will take SO much work!

   Then I'll actually have to start producing
      something!

Sit with your negative attitudes or fears about what you want. Focus on them with all your energy. FEEL what it means to be selfish, or how hard it will be to clean out that office. Notice how your body feels. Notice your emotions. Notice where your motivation goes.

III. Now, do a freewrite in the present tense in which you take at least three of these negative attitudes and do/think/feel the opposite, focusing on the positive.

Example:

> *I make an extra strong pot of coffee on a Saturday when everybody is out of the house. I open all the windows, turn the volume way up on my favorite music, and throw on some funky clothes. I don't do any other errands first; I just tackle that room. My goal is to have a cleaned out room by the end of this day. Whatever I don't get to, I'll come back to it next Saturday, and the following one until this room is mine again.*

Compare the two feeling states and see which one makes you feel inspired and motivated to have the very thing you desire. Feeling inspired and motivated are signposts pointing, "GO THIS WAY!"

CHAPTER EIGHT

Quick Tricks to Positivity

There are two ways of meeting difficulties: you alter the difficulties or you alter yourself to meet them.

—Phyllis Bottome

Jordan writes:

I try to latch onto positive feelings whenever they strike and use them as a platform from which to draw other desires to me. I often seek out environments where I know I will feel good. One such place is a Northern California retreat center where I have both led and attended retreats.

In January 2006, exhausted from working on a series of complicated and time-consuming projects, I took advantage of a weekend retreat that was being offered at a discount due to the season.

I had numerous ideas of what to work on while there but knew I had to choose one thing and focus on it. In my writing practice I have discovered that even a couple of days with unadulterated time, free of e-mail and phone calls, offers a window in which to accomplish things that have been put off. So I brought something new with me that kept buzzing at my subconscious, but which I hadn't yet made time to work on—a proposal for a book to instruct writers on how to write powerful scenes.

I arrived at the retreat center on a drizzly Friday afternoon. A delicate, steamy fog drifted off the foliage and the evergreens seemed even more alive against the gray clouds. By Saturday the drizzle had turned to a gentle but persistent rain, forcing me to stay inside and write.

I couldn't help but appreciate the simple things during my stay, such as having my meals prepared for me, or the sound of the swollen river rushing below. I fell in love with the simple task of making and tending a fire every day, which I was unable to do at home. I paid keen attention to details I often fail to notice—the way the sunlight broke through the clouds, or the beauty of silence—and funneled all this appreciation and joy into the book proposal I was eager to write. At the end of two days I had a rough proposal that I felt energized about, as if it was created out of the scent of evergreens and wood smoke.

When I returned home, I put this product into the computer and sent it off to the acquisitions editor of Writer's Digest Books.

I heard from them within a week; they were interested and felt my book had unique potential to reach their book club audience. The editors at *Writer's Digest* and I refined my idea so they could submit it at their next proposal meeting. Whenever I wondered what they thought or got caught up in a state of anxiety I returned to my images of the weekend retreat, where the proposal was born, allowing the lingering smell of wood smoke and loamy earth to filter into my senses and remind me how wonderful it had been.

A month and a half later I got the good news. Writer's Digest accepted my proposal and I was given a contract to write my first published book, *Make A Scene: Crafting a Powerful Story One Scene at a Time.* I still credit that powerful, simple weekend and all the small ways I felt my spirits uplifted, for putting me in the perfect feeling state to make it happen.

Where and how you focus your attention is also where and how you create space for your life in general, and your specific desires. Your thoughts and feelings form a unique magnet that only you possess. Each person has their own version of this magnet, comprised of all the thoughts and feelings that go into your personal mix. If you are sitting down to your desk with an attitude of positive anticipation, excited to start a new plan to write a page a day, chances are that particular sitting is going to go pretty well. You're more likely to write something you'll want to keep, maybe the beginnings of a novel, a poem or an essay.

Say you go to visit a friend who is in a really bad mood from a terrible day. Notice what happens if you start to commiserate and share your own examples of bad news. You start to feel lousy, and quickly, lousy little events, people, and circumstances start trickling your way. This chapter is designed to give you a few quick and easy tricks for attracting positivity to you when you need it fast. Think of these activities like little energy bursts, designed to power you up in moments when you aren't feeling positive, or when you want to take a state of positivity and jazz it up even higher.

We're trained to believe that we should only be so happy, as if there is a certain level of happiness that is criminal and for which we will be punished. After playing with the activities in this section, you're apt to experience what it feels like to be as happy as you possibly can, even if only for a few moments. Eventually you can learn to sustain positivity for longer and longer periods of time and with it, begin attracting all the things you hoped and longed for in your writing life.

ACTIVITIES

✍ Calibrating Your Magnet

From here on out, think of your feeling states as your "magnet," and be aware that whatever you're feeling creates a vibrational pull. Our wish for you is that you recognize what comes to you as being in direct relationship to your "magnetic" vibration. This is not to say that you are responsible for all the things that happen in life, but you will probably notice that the more finely calibrated your magnet is toward positivity, the less other people's problems, crises, and troubles will come directly your way.

I. Take a glance back at "The Feeling List" in Chapter Three. Where are you on that list right now? How do you know that's where you are? What cues—physical, emotional, or otherwise—point to how you feel? What events or circumstances have led up to your feeling this state?

Example:

I am at number 4, "Hopeful/Optimistic/Expectant."

I know that's where I am because I feel a tingle of excitement in my sternum, which I always get when I am looking forward to something.

The reasons for this feeling of hopeful excitement are, one, my birthday is in a couple of days, so I am specifically looking forward to something that I expect will be fun, and I have high hopes that my family might do something special for me. Two, I'm also feeling hopeful because I mailed off a short story to a publication that feels like the right place for it, and I visualized an acceptance before

I sent it, as well as meditated myself into a state
of blissful anticipation before I did so. Three, I'm
feeling hopeful that my husband will get this job
he interviewed for.

<u>Some tips</u>: Though we're asking you to write this down the first time you do it, the goal is to entertain this activity at any moment when you are feeling uncertain, muddled, or confused and ask yourself, "What am I feeling? Why? How did I get to this feeling place?" On the other hand, when you already feel good, and don't want to dip down to a lower feeling state, you can use this same game to keep yourself buzzing high.

It's rare that we stop and take the time to understand WHY we feel a certain way. The point in doing so is to help us recreate scenarios that made us feel good and recognize the direct link between feelings and what happens to us.

After awhile it will feel hard to identify if your good feelings led to good circumstances, or if good circumstances led to good feelings. At that point, rejoice; you've achieved enough of your desires that both your feelings and the things happening in your life are good!

✍ Gushing Gratitude

How many times in a day do you stop to think of those things you are grateful for? And not just "things" but people, states of mind, situations, actions done on your behalf and more?

Gratitude is a powerful feeling because it sends the message that you are happy about something that you already have, therefore drawing more happiness to you. Gratitude is the absolute opposite of longing, which is a hollow, desperate feeling, and guaranteed to create more of the same in your life.

We often tend to be grateful for dramatic acts and large gestures: gifts, life-saving moments, emergency help, and the like. We often forget to be grateful for the things that are with us on a daily basis, but which we wouldn't want to do without. In this game, you'll get a chance to exercise your gratitude over a continuum from the very small to the expansively large.

I. Situate yourself somewhere that you will stay for the duration of this exercise. Drawing from only that which you can SEE, write down ten things in your sight that you are or could be grateful for. Then list why you are grateful for them.

Example:

1. *My hole punch. Why? Because I have lots of things to put into binders and this hole punch means I don't have to go to the copy center or borrow someone else's. It's always there when I need it.*

2. *A potted plant. I feel that plants always add a dimension of extra life and energy. This one in particular is so persistent in growing despite how often I water it.*

3. *A pair of flip-flops. These are the most comfortable flip-flops I have ever owned, and they make my feet happy on hot days.*

4. *A bottle of purple ink. I love the color purple; it brightens my mood. I'm grateful that it brightens up my journal writing experience.*

5. *Scissors. I am grateful for my scissors because I'm always cutting out articles or lists of things, and I'm never more aware of how much I need them than when someone has borrowed them and I can't find them.*

II. Now make a second list of five people you are grateful for and why.

III. Then make a third list of ten nonmaterial things that you are grateful for (such as: "Creativity, my good sense of humor, my husband's kindness, meditation") and why.

Some tips: Don't dwell too much on the "why." Let the first answer that comes to your mind be the answer you write down. Often we are grateful for something for very simple reasons, but those reasons are no less noble than anything we have put complicated thought into. A color, a word of kindness, these things reach beyond the intellectual mind into the body, the heart, and the soul and speak to those parts of us directly.

When you have completed these three lists, notice how you feel just by the effort of having stopped to think about what you are grateful for. Let yourself stay in that high-quality, finely tuned state of being for at least one minute. What you've just done can be practiced in the car on the way to work, during a stressful business meeting, while waiting in a long line at the store, or even during an argument. The trick is to find something to be grateful for where you are at any given moment.

We recommend that you start every day with a quick written list of what you're grateful for that day. You'll be amazed how quickly it can pull you up to the highest tip of the feeling list.

✍ Pocket Pronouncements

This activity is perhaps the simplest, most basic one in the entire book. It is one of the most important, too, because it is a daily reminder, something you can do every day.

As a writer you have a direct and magnificent line of communication with the universe. When you write something down, you begin a process of setting things into motion. The moment you jot down what you want, you send a message out to the universe that is heard instantly.

Writing has the power to undo and redo. We played with this some in the storytelling and revising chapters, but it is the truth upon which the Write Free work is built. Writing really can free you. Even if you can only take the tiniest step toward a goal, by simply writing down what you want, you are already on your way.

I. This activity is one we hope you will do as often as you can, returning to it over and over again. In a place where you can easily look at it throughout the day, write the following:

Today I purposely and intentionally notice how I feel, focus on what I want, and recognize that through writing, I will make space for my creative life and desires.

Now fill in the blanks:

1. *Today I intend:*

2. *Today I am grateful for:*

3. *Today I have absolute certainty that:*

4. *Today I am proud of:*

5. *Today I trust:*

6. *Today I give:*

7. *Today I celebrate:*

We call these "Pocket Pronouncements" because you should be able to write them on something small enough to carry around with you, yet their size and power is far greater than you imagine. Each time you do this, you add energy to your magnet and create a routine of positivity that builds and builds on itself in ways you should continue to be able to see in your life.

CHAPTER NINE

The Write Way

We must become the change we want to see in the world.

—Mohandas K. Gandhi

Jordan writes:

Some months ago I received the sweetest e-mail unexpectedly from a woman named Rhiannon in North Carolina. She had read an article of mine published in *The Writer* magazine. She wrote: "When I see a piece of art, including writing that moves me, I make a point to get in touch with the artist/author and let them know and/or share their work with others. You did a great job and I thank you for inspiring me!"

I was impressed by Rhiannon's sincerity and her genuine enthusiasm; it's nice to know your work has made an impression, and even nicer when readers go out of their way to tell you so. We quickly struck up an e-mail friendship. The power of attraction is a tremendous force; even when you don't know that it's working, it is. Rhiannon is building a freelance writing life for herself, and in the course of these past few months, her stories of success so impressed me, I asked her to take an inventory of how her good feelings had laid down the cobblestones to her ultimate desire. Rhiannon writes the following:

"I've always been a writer. I read and hear other writers say this over and over and over. Some of us feel writing is as much a part of our being as our fingers and toes; we know from the beginning. I am no different. More than a compulsion to spread my words on the pages, arranging them just so, I am driven to present my words to others; I need to be read. I create and allow opportunities for others to explore my words.

"Involved in my community as a girl, I wrote plays for friends to perform before family and neighbors. Later, as section leader in the high school band, I wrote and issued *The Flutey News* to keep my little group organized and excited during our busy football and concert seasons. When an issue involving our school struck me I would submit an article to the school newspaper inevitably making the front page of the next edition.

"When deciding on a major for college my first thought was journalism. Being young and impressionable, I allowed others to sway me into a business concentration and became the manager of my school's off-campus bookstore. Impetuous and competitive, I used my writing skills, and that school's paper, to attract business.

"More recently I told my boss I intended to become an expert in the field by writing articles for industry trade journals. He laughed. But before long, an article I wrote was published regionally and then nationally. My boss stopped laughing and started bragging.

"Lately I have created so many writing opportunities I can barely keep up—and I love every moment of it. The more I explore the writing world, the more opportunities I see, request, and receive.

"I have found my rightful path again: I am a student

once more, pursuing a degree in journalism. I have secured positions as a staff writer on both the official school paper, and the alternate school paper, as an editor. I am nearly ten years older than the rest of the staff. The editors feel I am 'experienced' and allow me free reign to write anything I wish; so far, every article has made print.

"Every time I decide I want to write for publication, an opportunity presents itself. When I concentrate on my goals, doors open. When I ask, I receive. Looking back I see it clearly: The path was always beneath my feet; all I had to do was put on my shoes."

If you have played with the activities in this book thus far, we wager that some changes have taken place in your life. We want to make sure that you don't let them pass by without a nod of recognition. The moment you become aware that direct play with feelings and visioning has an effect in the material world, the more inclined you'll be to keep it up. You have the potential to revise the way you look at your entire life. Things no longer have to "just happen" to you. You need not be a victim of circumstance or perpetually in resistance or longing. You can walk through life with the knowledge that you are actively, purposely attracting the writing life you have always dreamed of.

Chapter Nine will give you some ways to measure the changes taking place in your life as a result of working with the energy of attraction. Once you can see the changes, chances are you will become motivated to start upping the stakes. Maybe you've asked for small things, taken only baby steps. Perhaps you haven't fully trusted that it was okay for you to have all that you really want. Chapter Nine will give you a chance to envision wider, ask for more, and stand in your own deserving with added confidence. Once you realize that the little things can change, you might just be inspired to attract the most amazing writing life you can possibly imagine.

ACTIVITIES

✍ Measuring

You may find you haven't yet reflected on the progress made as a result of doing the activities in this book. Perhaps you've done the exercises, tucked them away, and pressed on. If you've fallen into the habit of working at these exercises, or doing them out of a sense of obligation, you might want to play some of the activities again with a sense of absolute whimsy, a sense of lightness and spontaneity. The better you feel while doing them, the better the results. Now it's time to take stock of how far you've come, and what stumbling blocks are left to clear from your path.

I. Make a simple list, off the top of your head, and ask yourself: What has changed in my life since I began working with this book? Put down anything that comes to mind on this list. Do a minimum of ten.

Example:

> *That difficult client stopped calling; I finally had that mole checked out; my mother stopped teasing me about getting a "real job;" a short story was accepted for publication; I let a trusted writing friend read my novel; I signed up for a writing class; I started regularly submitting my work once a month.*

II. Now make a second, similar, list, and ask yourself: What has stayed the same? Use this to refer to things you had hoped to change, not just things that were likely to stay the same.

Example:

> *I'm still not a published novelist; I haven't quit my grueling day job yet; I haven't cleaned out my desk to make it easier to write.*

III. Now look at that last list of things that haven't happened yet. Have you made any strides in the direction of the items on the list? Though the goal may not have been achieved, have any stepping-stones been established?

Example:

> *Well, I did start querying literary agents. I told my boss that if I don't get a raise in the next six months, I may have to consider leaving; I have taken to writing in the living room, which is cozier than my office space.*

IV. After reviewing both lists, ask yourself: Which did I focus on more—those things that are changing, or those things that are staying the same?

Example:

> *It's hard for me not to focus on what I don't have. I'm much more aware of absence than I am of what I have.*

<u>Some tips</u>: If you find yourself focusing more on a lack than what has come to you, shifted or changed, you're not alone. But let us remind you: Where you place your attention, what you focus on, is where and how you create your life. If you are prone to noticing lack, then don't be surprised if you still find you have more lack than fullness. However, don't disqualify the huge power of attraction. The places you have focused positively have overridden

years of negativity and paved the way for good things to come to you. It's all about balance. The more time you spend focusing on what you want—not out of longing, but out of a joyous feeling that having what you want makes you feel good—the more it will come to you.

✍ Amplifying

However high you've aimed for your desires thus far, get ready. We're going to ask you to aim EVEN HIGHER. If you thought you were asking for big things, get ready to expand your vision once more.

I. Make a list of ten things you desire that you have NOT YET written down as a result of one of our activities. Reach big. This is where you get to envision running the United Nations, inventing a new clean form of energy, living in a mansion atop a sprawling hundred-acre property, or owning your own small island. In this exercise you are especially encouraged to suspend all judgments of what you want. Grow your desires as big as you possibly can. Don't hold back.

Example:

> 1. *I want to be such a successful novelist that all my books are optioned into movies, and celebrities clamor to read my next book just to see if they want to star in it.*
>
> 2. *I want to have my own television program interviewing writers.*
>
> 3. *I want to be so wealthy that I have millions of dollars at my disposal.*

II. Look at each item on that list and get honest with yourself. What do you feel when you look at your desire? Proud? Ashamed? Afraid of being "found out"? Thrilled with yourself for coming up with that idea? The more honest you are, the easier you can move on to the next activity.

III. Once you've identified how each of your biggest, wildest dreams makes you feel when you see it written down, start a fresh list of five reasons why the realization of each desire would BENEFIT the world. That's five reasons for EACH desire.

Example:

> *I want to have my own television program interviewing writers. With a forum like television at my disposal, I could create unique programs to foster literacy in this country. I could get to know important people and encourage them to inspire others. I could counteract some of the poor programming on TV. I could show that reading is a worthy endeavor.*

<u>Some tips</u>: The minute you tell yourself you can't/ shouldn't/ought not/won't have what you desire, you limit the possibilities. You stop your inner magnet from attracting the good, limiting yourself to whatever small spectrum of desires you feel you deserve.

When you achieve a goal, or realize a desire, what happens is something altogether unexpected, alchemical...it leads to other, better things you could not have envisioned or even known to have desired for yourself. When you realize one goal, a whole new world of possibilities opens up. To tap into the forces of attraction is an endlessly creative process, but it begins with you allowing yourself to stretch wide open in the scope of your desires.

✍ Joy on Demand

We'd like you to keep a notebook that has only one purpose: To be an inventory of all that gives you joy. This book will be ongoing, and you may find that you wind up with more than one, even multiple, inventories over time.

I. Every day (or as often you can) go to your Joy Inventory and write down everything that gives you joy. Nothing is too small, and nothing too large. From the smell of a certain kind of soap to good news about your writing, the Joy Inventory can hold everything. Also consider writing down words that give you joy and make you feel happy. As writers, our medium is language; it improves our craft to notice those bits of language that inspire us as well.

Example:

8/31/2005: The texture of oatmeal. My tiger lily when she blooms. Meyer lemons. A really good independent movie. Scratching an itch. The words gravid and orison.

<u>Some tips</u>: What goes into your Joy on Demand notebook need not have come from that particular day. The idea is teach yourself to notice the entire scope of that which brings you joy so that you can learn to rely less on "big" events, and find joy in small ways throughout a given day. The more joy you can find in the world around you, "on demand" so to speak, the more power you are giving to that magnet of yours to attract more of the good stuff.

II. Now, when you're really in need of a joy fix, or when you want to take a good feeling state and raise it to its highest level, take any one thing from your Joy on Demand notebook, something that resonates with you, and freewrite about it:

Example:

> *The texture of oatmeal gives me joy because it is so primal, comforting, and reminds me of all the meals my mother used to make for me when I was little; it reminds me of how cared for I felt, and how there is no care like a mother's. There's something about the feeling of oatmeal that is soft like a blanket, or like my cat's fur, something that says, "you are safe, you are comforted." All it takes is the feel of oatmeal in my mouth to elicit this wide range of comforting, happy feelings in me.*

On your way out the door, or before you start any given day, try to look at your Joy on Demand notebook, no matter what page, and carry a few items of joy with you wherever you go.

Write Free

PART FOUR

WRITING FREE!

Deliberately writing your deepest desires

All the learning you've done so far comes to bear on this final part of the book. By identifying what you don't want, you've cleared space for your deepest desires. You've learned to let go of negative feelings that block your good. You've planned for your desires and felt your story. You're also wiser and more aware of how your feelings affect your life. Now is your chance to feel the fullness of deliberately creating your good. There is power, growth, and joy in developing awareness, so take a moment to feel how far you've come. You've earned it!

In Part Four, we invite you to continue to Write Free, to do your creative work with joy and inspiration. These final chapters are reminders that your life is a manifestation of the energy you flow. Knowing this, you can go forward with the confidence that comes with having your deepest desires. How or when your desires become reality is not up to you, but feeling their reality is. Your confidence that your wishes will be fulfilled—indeed, are fulfilled—signals the universe that your deepest desires are coming true.

Open yourself to the power of your feelings as you write the activities in the following chapters. Allow them to be full and rich inside you. They will empower you to do your work, and, perhaps even better, understand the rewards of writing free without fear.

CHAPTER TEN

Wishing and Hoping

Hope begins in the dark, the stubborn hope that if you just show up and try to do the right thing, the dawn will come.

—Anne Lamott

Rebecca writes:

For decades, I'd kept daily journals, matter-of-fact logs of the day's activities. A few years ago, already in possession of a few milk crates full of these journals, I decided to glean material for a book of essays. As I took steps to write the essays, collect them in a book-length manuscript, and find an agent, I worked with a professional coach for whom I wrote laundry lists of weekly tasks to accomplish. The lists focused my energy, and as I reviewed them at the end of each week, I found many of the tasks had been completed effortlessly. Sometimes it was the action of others, unasked, that finished the needed work. I came to call my list for each week The Wish List (see Activities, this chapter).

Soon after discovering the potential of The Wish List, I began meeting with Jordan regularly to talk about writing. After a few meetings, we both decided to use The Wish List to keep track of our writing intentions. Convening near our mutual workplace, escaping the indoors, we'd sit near a lovely creek to share our lists. With the creek song nearby, at a table in the shade of the willows, we'd marvel not only at how much we desired, but also at how much we'd easily achieved. Focusing on our writing lives while in a light, joyful state enlivened our feelings and gave us energy to achieve our dreams. Recording tasks on The Wish List and returning to it weekly seemed to get any job done.

✿

Wishes are powerful urges. They come from deep within and, when not suppressed, have much to say about how we long to live our lives. Wishes are like clouds towering on the horizon saying, "Notice me." If we ignore such auspicious warnings, even basic needs such as physical comfort go unmet. If we pay attention and prepare for the coming weather, however, inclement conditions cease to be a problem, and they also can bring energy and excitement. The same could be said for wishes: pay attention to them, prepare for them, and you will enjoy the rewards.

Wishes come with big packets of feeling energy attached. Say you've had your eye on a magazine in which you'd like to publish your work. You can approach it several ways: one, with certainty that you'll find a way into its pages if it's right for you, or two, with hopelessness and doubt. Which attitude do you think inspires the kind of action that produces positive results? Which attitude leads to contacting the right editor, writing with vision and imagination, and sending the best work you have to offer? It all starts with a wish; it continues with inspired action supporting the wish.

In the preceding chapters, you've learned to identify some of your deepest wishes. In this chapter, you will learn writing tools that turn wishes and hopes into reality.

When your feelings are in a state of high vibration, you attract life situations of a similar high vibration. When you act in support of a deep wish or passion, you are shooting for the stars. Your heart is full and alive! Aiming high is more likely to propel you into orbit than targeting a low-vibration goal (for you) or not taking aim at all.

Who knows? You may just hit the stars you aim for—or at least the lofty, beautiful air of the peaks in between heaven and earth.

ACTIVITIES

✍ Dream Journal

Writers tend to have writerly hopes and dreams. The sweeter those hopes and dreams, the sweeter the writer's life will be. This game allows you to translate your dream energy directly to the page. The technique described below came to us from the late William Everton, a respected poet who taught dream-based poetry classes for many years. We discovered from his work that tuning into our dreams contributed to our writing lives; to this technique we added describing our feelings upon waking. We include this game here because we think it's important to pay attention to as many clues as possible when seeking to understand your emotional life.

I. Designate journal space specifically for recording your dreams. You can devote pages in your Write Free journal, or you can use a new journal dedicated entirely to your dreams.

II. Keep the journal and a pen next to your bed when you go to sleep at night. It helps to keep a flashlight handy or have a lamp nearby that you can switch on, if needed, in the dark.

III. Sleep as you normally do, and if you have lingering images of your dreams upon waking, record them. This may require sitting up, turning on the light, and working with sleepy eyes. When you first try it, you may have just a few images to record. You may remember only a color, or that music was playing in your dream, or that a friend or relative was with you. Don't worry that you don't know what anything means. Just jot down the images.

IV. Beside the images you've noted, write a word or two that describes your feeling upon waking.

You may feel hopeful, fortunate, sad, or lonely. Find one word to describe your mood and write it in the margin of your journal page.

Some tips: It's best to work when you first awaken. It doesn't matter how fleeting the dream images are—try to capture at least a sense of them on paper. The process can take less than one minute a day. And, like anything, your ability to keep a dream journal will improve with practice. It's not important that you write a detailed testimonial of your dreams—what's important is that you note them. Soon you'll be remembering more of your subconscious life. It may also seem that you'll be dreaming more.

Writing dream images while in a deeply relaxed state will also add riches to your writing. The images that come to you will be fodder for your imagination, whether or not you ever even return to your journal to reread the images.

Try this game for two weeks and see if you don't get hooked!

✍ The Bookshelf Game

Even inanimate objects seem to carry energy that affects your life. A kitchen table may remind you of good times, for instance, or a living room couch may bring back a difficult phase in your past. Similarly, the books you own speak volumes about the life you've lived until now. Their vibrational energy, like that of any object, will attract certain experiences to you.

You may be a writer who'd like to have a dozen published books to her credit. Playing this game with the books you already own could be just the way to manifest that desire.

I. Select one shelf that you'd like to see filled with your own books. If you don't have a piece of furniture with multiple shelves, don't worry. You can play this game with the books on your writing desk or on the nightstand beside your bed.

II. Arrange the books in order of importance to you. Start with your favorite one. Perhaps it's one you wish you'd written yourself. Place it on the far left or right side of your shelf. Next to it, place your second favorite, your third favorite after that, and so on. As you arrange the books, make a mental note of one or more you'd like to add to the collection. These will be your books, those you write yourself and have published. See them on the shelf beside those you already own. Say to yourself, "And so it is!"

Some tips: This game evolved from the feng shui principle of arranging furniture and decorative items in your home in accordance with the energy you wish to attract. Do your framed pictures stand alone, isolated from others? Do you have glass figurines standing apart? If so, you're probably attracting solo energy. To be in a couple, we're told to cluster our objects in pairs. To be in a family, we arrange them in groups of three or more. It's the same with our books—to be a writer of books you value, start by grouping those you already own. They'll attract other excellent books, including some you write yourself. Try this game and watch your collection of your own novels, anthologies, and chapbooks grow!

✍ The Wish List

This is the game that started it all! The Wish List is a simple grid with amazing powers. Writing your intentions in The Wish List lifts your energy about them and mobilizes help in all forms. All it takes to get started is a pen, your journal, and your deep desires.

I. Open your journal to a clean, two-page spread. Write the date in an upper corner. Recording the date is essential. You'll want a record of when you began this game, for comparison to later Wish Lists.

II. On the left page, create two columns for the full length of the page. Label the first column "1 Month" and the second "3 Months." On the right page, create two more columns. Label the first column "6 Months" and the second "1 Year."

III. In each column, list your vision of what you wish to have in your life during those time periods. Don't worry about how you're to achieve your wishes. Just honor that you want something, and note that you intend to manifest it.

Example:

1 Month	3 Months	6 Months	1 Year
Write every morning	Assemble three morning writings into essays	Publish at least three essays in journals of my choice	Enjoy status as author with several published essays to my credit

<u>Some tips</u>: Play this game slowly and with an awareness of your feelings as you go. Allow yourself a minute as you record each intention. Then set aside The Wish List. You can check back in time to see how you've done. You'll be astounded at how "on schedule" you are! But please don't worry about "missing deadlines." The Wish List is not a list of deadlines. If you don't hit the intentions in the time frames listed, you simply get to reframe the timeline. The Wish List is meant to be refreshed as often as needed to renew feelings about goals. More often than not, you'll be amazed at how often the intentions have become reality, and not so far off from the proposed time. But don't take our word for it. Try it for yourself!

CHAPTER ELEVEN

Engaging Your Desire

*Right action is freedom
From past and future also.*

—T. S. Eliot

Rebecca writes:

Another example of attracting the creative life is this story my friend Elizabeth shared with me just this morning. She'd been working with her attitudes toward abundance in a low-key, no-pressure way: "I'd been meditating every morning in the usual way, just watching my breath and relaxing my mind. Each day for forty days I also reminded myself that I wanted money to come to me, out of nowhere, so I could have time to write and still contribute needed income to my family. Some large, juicy sum of money."

Elizabeth wanted this money to help support her while she finished writing her sixth novel. The previous five novels were still sitting in her files, unpublished. Although she'd worked with an agent in the past, she was not currently represented. She had a feeling, however, that the support the desired money would bring her would buy freedom and space to engage in a deeper, more creative writing process that would make the sixth novel the one that attracted a new agent who could sell her work.

"I began to ask the universe for $4,000," Elizabeth told me. "Then, one morning, I decided to double my request. I simply changed my thinking to 'Really, $8,000 would be more helpful.' Doubling it was my way of allowing myself to have more abundance in my life. I didn't have a huge attachment to any of the particulars. I just kind of thought, 'Wouldn't it be nice if this happened?' And I wrote it down, just as the words flowed to me. Then I went about my days in the usual way, novel writing in the morning and editing the manuscripts of others in the afternoons.

"You will not believe what John and I got in the mail today," she e-mailed me this morning. "It had been forwarded from our old address: a refund check from the U.S. Treasury for $8,000. I am not kidding. So in trying to decide where it came from we went back and looked at our taxes. We'd been pretty surprised in April to find we owed money to the IRS when we'd already paid so much withholding through the year. Our tax return showed almost nothing for our withholding. I hadn't been able to figure it out, so I'd taken the position of 'my accountant knows best' and didn't follow up.

"Turns out, our accountant had entered the wrong amount of withholding! The IRS corrected the return and sent us our refund. Guess what date the check is dated? June 9th. The very day I decided to end my personal forty-day abundance program."

Time and again we find that we attract exactly what we ask for.

✧

A signboard posted at one of our local churches reads, "If God is your co-pilot, switch seats." Referring to a well-known book of similar name, the sign reminds us that we can delegate a large part of the steering required for our life's journey. Why not ally with the greater forces that are at work in your life? The metaphysical literature claims that mere seconds of directed, feeling energy marshals the universe's forces toward your desired outcome. Try feeling for a whole minute! You're flowing energy toward your results anyway, whether you like it or not, so being aware of the energy you flow is simply taking charge of your good. In this chapter you'll learn to join with the forces you need to get where you're going.

Attracting what you want does take action. To be a writer, for example, you must undertake the action of writing. To be a published author, at some point you must seek publishers. These actions are logical steps toward desired goals. They determine the day-to-day activity of what you are to become. Your feelings as you go about taking the actions, however, determine the results.

In this chapter you'll learn to write your feelings in ways that signal your various co-pilots to take their seats and do their part of the flying.

ACTIVITIES

✍ Activity Log

Remember, how you feel as you take action toward your desires determines the results. Over the next two weeks, or over another time period of your choosing, use this log as a record of your feelings while you take action regarding a specific desire of yours.

I. Write a list of five of your greatest desires.

Example:

1. *To be a published novelist*

2. *To marry and live happily ever after*

3. *To prosper greatly from my creative endeavors*

4. *To travel around the world*

5. *To always have wonderful friends*

II. Next, choose one or two desires to focus on over the next two weeks (or time period of your choosing).

Example:

To be a published novelist

Let your feelings guide you to which desires to work on first. They don't have to be the greatest wishes, although we recommend that you take steps toward your biggest desires as soon as you're ready.

III. In your journal, dedicate a full page to this game. Write "Activity Log" at the top of the page and "Become a Published Novelist" below it.

Set up the page for the log. Create three columns. Label them from left to right: "Date," "My Inspired Action," and "How I Felt Doing It."

IV. Each day during your chosen period, log one action toward your desire.

Example: *To be a published novelist*

Date	My Inspired Action	How I Felt Doing It
Nov. 15	*Looked at structure of favorite novels*	*Focused, happy*

You may wish to log more than one action, and this is fine, but the simpler you keep your log, the more apt you are to continue keeping it. Make it an intention to enter a single entry in your log every day.

Some tips: Some of your actions may feel bigger than others. Calling an agent, for example, may feel more important to you than writing a paragraph of your novel as you prepare it for publication. All actions add up to the final result, however, and if you are flowing good feelings as you take each of these actions, they will add up to more than the sum of their parts. Remember, an action can be as simple as writing down what you want. If you're performing the action with inspired feelings, you'll be astounded by its results.

✍ Ten Things I Love to Do

Here is another deceptively simple activity. Again it can be played even when time is limited, with good results.

I. Make a list of ten things you feel good doing. Keep it very simple—use no more than three words for each item.

Example:

1. *Write*
2. *Enjoy my family*
3. *Cook*
4. *Garden*
5. *Play music*
6. *Converse*
7. *Swim*
8. *Shop for antiques*
9. *Bicycle*
10. *Explore new places*

It's okay to write this list quickly, without worrying about the order of the items.

II. Next, quickly write a list of how you feel you actually do spend your time.

Example:

1. *Work*
2. *Clean up*
3. *Attend meetings*

4. *Eat*

5. *Do chores*

6. *Converse*

7. *Cook*

8. *Swim/bicycle*

9. *Walk*

10. *Run errands*

This list does not have to be accurate. In the final chapter of this book, we'll learn a method that tells us just how we spend our time. For now, this list is about your perceptions. And again, it doesn't have to be in any particular order.

III. Pick one item from the first list to focus on now. Close your eyes and spend a minute feeling the feeling.

Example:

How I Spend My Time: *Write*

Feelings When I Spend My Time This Way:

Deep, like my creative well is bottomless

Feel the sensation of sitting down at your desk with an idea in mind. How does it feel to get the idea on paper, watch it take shape as your subconscious helps you go to work on it, and read it later? Journal these feelings if you wish.

<u>Some tips</u>: That's all there is to it. Don't spend much time pondering the second list, which notes how you actu-

ally feel you spend your time. You'll return to the second list later, simply to gauge how far you've come since you wrote it. It's fun to compare the two, but it's the first list that deserves your feeling attention. It's good to return to this game regularly, to see what's changed in your "current activities" list.

✍ Journal Boogie

Ever notice how an empty dance floor invites more emptiness, whereas just one person getting out there and dancing invites more dancers? Engaging your desires is like boogying with the universe: if you let it know when to show up, it will be a good dance partner. Sometimes the act of notifying the universe of its daily part in the dance is as simple as writing down its roles, as we do in this activity.

I. Open your journal to a clean page. Divide it into two columns. Draw a single line down the center of the page. At the top, label the left column "My Tasks" and the second "Ask Tasks."

II. Fill in the left column with tasks you absolutely must do today. These are your drop-dead deadlines. Have a closing date at work? Write it down. Need to get a check to the bank today? Write "Bank." Keep it brief and do-able. Don't get stuck, just keep the hand moving, as with a good freewrite.

III. In the right column, write other tasks you'd accomplish if you've got time today. These are tasks that also must be accomplished, but they're too huge to be taken on today or they're a little further into the future.

Write Free

Example:

My Tasks	Ask Tasks
Finish and mail report	*Find new employee to help with future reports*
Type in new chapter of book	*Finish the book*

Some tips: The Ask Tasks are those to be accomplished with the help of the Universe. Writing them to the right of the line is equivalent to asking the Universe to support you in getting them done. Writing them there rather than on your very action-oriented "To-Do" list raises your "Help Wanted" vibrations to a level of attraction that brings assistance raining in on you.

CHAPTER TWELVE

Allowing Your Good

But we are now admitted to the banquets of the gods;
We may deal with the laws of heaven above . . .

—Edmond Halley

Rebecca writes:

During a particularly stressful time last month, I was expressing my frustration about life's difficulties in inappropriate ways. Negative thoughts filled my tired soul, and those were the thoughts that came out in my speech. In my feeling of overwhelm, I forgot to engage the activities in this book—I simply was not caring for myself in ways needed to keep up with the busy life I was living. I could sense my loved ones turning away from me, and it wasn't what I wanted for my life—in fact it was the least desirable outcome I could imagine for my relationships with family and friends.

One practice I still adhered to religiously, however, was Meditation (see Activities, this chapter). I did it merely out of habit, remembering from long experience how essential it is. Like everything else at that time, I felt I didn't have time for it. Still, thankfully, I meditated every morning and a few evenings as well.

One morning after a particularly stressful day and rugged night's sleep, I sat down as usual to meditate. I'd been feeling at the limit of my energy for days, and relations at home and work felt strained. I saw in myself unattractive patterns of behavior and despaired over whether I'd ever change. Drastic measures were needed.

As I meditated, an idea came to me as naturally and easily as breathing. I could take a Vow of Silence. Much as monks and others in holy retreat make huge lifestyle changes to enlighten their souls, I could do the same at home. I'd be in silence much of the time, and I'd share my thoughts when asked, but I was through dumping verbiage and opinions on others without invitation.

In the days that followed, peace entered my spirit. I had as many commitments as I'd had the weeks before, and I worked to keep up with them as always, but my Vow of Silence prevented me from leaking unintentionally harmful words to others. I found it easier to cope with each day's demands because the vow met my needs as an introvert. To maintain my vow, I found myself naturally caring for myself better. As a result, I had more energy to care for my loved ones as well.

This method works for me, although I'm sure I would not have thought of it without the deep insight and rest I get from meditation.

Now you've arrived at the final chapter of the book. You've reached the best part: allowing your good. "Allow" comes from French roots: *allouer*, to approve. Allowing merely means approving of the changes in our lives and letting them flow. Allowing can be the most simple of all the steps we take to manifest our desires, but it can also be the most simple to mess up. Who among us has not meddled too much, trying to force an outcome, believing we know best? We're all human; we can't help but stick our spoons into the pot to stir the soup. If we don't like how things are going at work, we may rearrange them, hoping to effect change. Sometimes our meddling worsens the situation.

To allow doesn't mean we become passive or give up doing good work. It means we do our best at all times, labor diligently and with intention, and know when to stop. We keep our hands off the outcome and let the Universe step up to the plate to do its job. We know when to let go and let our good come to us without choking off the supply.

We writers have a unique opportunity to allow abundance to flow to us. As soon as we take up the pen, we tap into a process that explores the deep well of our subconscious. When we're writing, we ride a flow of energy and excitement. The act itself in such times of our lives is its own reward. Today, this very day, you may just be getting started in your writing life, finding your voice. Or, conversely, you've been at the writing life for a while and are about to receive yet another paycheck for pulling words out of the air. All stages of the process are wonderful. Keeping your focus on what's good about where you are today is the best way to reap further rewards.

Now is the time to allow appreciation for the good that is already in your writing and your life. Now is the time to flow energy to yourself and others, to approach your work with a joyous heart and loving hands. Love your life, approve of it, nurture it, practice caring for it, and your good will come.

The activities in this chapter will relax you and allow in not only the muse but the life coach within you—the first bringing bold, fresh ideas and the other patting your back and saying, "nice job."

ACTIVITIES

✍ Meditation: The Happening Silence

This activity is recommended by nearly every self-help program in the world. Open a book that promises a better life and you're bound to see meditation listed as a method for self-improvement. There's a reason for that. There's nothing more powerful than the inspiration that comes from a relaxed mind.

Seasoned meditators will tell you that in the silence of meditation, much happens. There's a lot going on in a body that's still as stone during meditation. This author learned to meditate thirty years ago, when as a college student I paid the student rate to learn Transcendental Meditation from a friend who'd recently been trained as an instructor. It was some of the best money I've ever spent on myself, my writing, my family, and my friends.

When you meditate, you relax enough to allow the subconscious to do its work in your writing and your life as the body/mind sinks to a deep level of quiet. Ideas come. Answers to questions sift out of the jumble of thoughts racing through your brain. In the silence, the tangled plot of a story you've been wrestling with sorts itself out. The character you've been struggling with changes her name. With your incoming breath, you solve the mystery of a word choice that hasn't seemed quite right.

If you already know how to meditate, commit yourself to daily practice. If you're new to meditation, follow the steps below. Take a few minutes each day, the same time of day if that works best for you. It may be the single best thing you do for your writing practice.

I. Sit in a quiet, comfortable place where you can easily see a clock or your watch.

Turn the ringer off on your phone. If you have a room to retreat to, it helps to have a "Meditating" sign on the door to ward off potential interruptions. Sitting in a chair or on a couch with a pillow to support your back is best. A floor pillow works fine, too, although you may want to lean up against a wall for back support. Sit tall but don't strain. It's important to be able to check the time during your meditation without straining or changing position. Being in view of a timepiece or setting a quiet alarm that won't startle you is helpful.

II. Close your eyes and settle in. As you relax, focus on the breath coming and going to and from your body.

Focusing on the breath keeps your attention inside your body. No need to be anxious about it, though. Just pay quiet attention to the sound and feel of inspiration and exhalation.

III. If your mind wanders, bring it back to your breath.

Our minds tend to stay very active in the beginning of this exercise. Have patience, stay with it, and soon your mind will be settled and more relaxed.

IV. End your meditation after twenty minutes. When you're ready, open your eyes and come back to full consciousness.

You can keep track of the time by opening one eye slightly if you have the sense that enough time has passed. When the twenty minutes have gone by, allow yourself to open your eyes, slowly, when you're ready. Pay attention to how you're feeling. You don't want to come out of the meditation too abruptly.

<u>Some tips</u>: You may be tempted to end your sitting before the time is fully up. Try to stay with it, though—teachers of meditation say you'll experience greater effect if you go a minimum of twenty minutes. It's good to journal about your experience immediately after meditation. Try following meditation up with ten minutes of journaling. What ideas came to you while sitting quietly? Get them down on paper.

Don't be discouraged if the results of meditation aren't immediately apparent to you. After you've been practicing for some time, you may start to notice how the plot of your novel will work out seemingly on its own, or the best idea for a business will come out of the air, or you'll decide what color to paint the living room. Never underestimate the power of the subconscious, especially if it's deeply relaxed.

As we feel, we experience. What better way to feel good than to know how to relax?

✍ Breathing In

Focusing on your breath can help you relax, as in the previous game, when you watched your breath in the process of meditation. Breath is also your inspiration. As you draw in breath, you draw in life. When you become aware that the very air you breathe is charged with your good, it's an easy leap to feeling the Universe lining up to support you.

This game seems uncomplicated in the extreme, but don't mistake its simplicity for simplemindedness. If you are able to tap into the good that surrounds you even in trying times, you have come far indeed.

This game can be played in a comfortable seated position (follow Step I in the previous game, Meditation, to prepare) or it can be played while walking, driving, or being otherwise occupied.

I. In your seated position, or while performing another activity, notice your feelings at this moment.

You may want to refer back to The Feeling List in Chapter Three. Are your emotions in a high, medium, or low vibration state? Just notice the sensation of your feelings right now.

II. Become aware of the breath entering and leaving your body.

As it enters feel each inspiration inflating your lungs, bringing life. Notice how good it is to be taking in oxygen from surroundings that support your good. As you exhale, simply let go of the breath in preparation to take in another lungful.

III. Continue for at least three minutes.

You can stop at any time, but preferably only after you've become aware of the improved feelings in your body.

Some tips: For an improved outlook, try this exercise when feeling low on The Feeling List. Or try it when you're feeling medium to high vibration but wouldn't mind feeling even more supported. It's effective in helping you prepare for a big event or meeting, at times of stress, or when time is limited for playing other activities. It has the immediate benefit of reminding us not to take wrong action but to pause and pursue only "inspired" action!

✍ Write Free

This last activity is as fun and beneficial as it gets. In it you get to play with poker chips, or coins, or toy building blocks, to actually schedule time to Write Free.

I. Gather 112 coins, poker chips, toy blocks, beads, or other small items that could be used for accounting for your time.

These markers will be used to represent the number of waking hours in your week. We've subtracted eight hours a day for sleeping, just for starters. Separate the markers into seven piles representative of the days of the week, Monday through Sunday. There should be sixteen markers in each pile.

II. Start with the Monday pile. Create four separate piles for groups of markers based on the following categories: Family/Relationships, Outside Work, Play/Exercise, and Creative Time.

Define each group as you see fit. Decide what is nonnegotiable and what can be cut into. Family/Relationships can be time with your spouse, child, or friends. Outside Work can be work performed outside the home for a steady paycheck, or it can be freelance writing assignments that must be pursued by phone, by e-mail, or in meetings. Play/Exercise can be your favorite activity with your church group, or it can be stopping by the pool for a swim. Assign markers to each group as you relate to it best.

We only ask that your Creative Time pile be thought of as your time for deep writing or other artistic pursuit, your time to play with characterizations in your fiction, or your writing practice time.

Start moving markers you already have information about, even if the category is not the most important to you. Are you expected to be at Outside Work for eight hours on Mondays? Set aside eight markers in your Outside Work pile.

III. Transfer your Creative Time into your weekly calendar. You can draw it in by hand on a paper calendar or add it to your computer timekeeper. Will the allotted hours work best in the morning before breakfast? Write it down. Do you write best in the evening? Record it.

Now that you've scheduled the Creative Time, it's yours to use. It's subject to re-evaluation at any time, of course. Just play the game again. But once it's on your calendar, until you change it again, it's sacred, structured time. Take the time to Write Free—you've earned it!

Some tips: Don't be discouraged if nothing comes of your Creative Time right away. No need to sabotage your work with unrealistic expectations. Trust that your good will come of it if you allow it to blossom. Seeing the time scheduled on your calendar will feel immensely satisfying and empowering for you. Such visioning is a powerful tool, because as you write, you manifest! Enjoy Writing Free your life.

Suggested Reading

We found the following references helpful as we researched and wrote the chapters in this book. It's up to us as writers to read—always read—to improve our craft. We hope you'll enjoy the time you spend exploring these selections.

Goldberg, Natalie. 1991. *Writing Down the Bones: Freeing the Writer Within*. New York: Quality Paperback Book Club.

Goldberg, Natalie. 2000. *Thunder and Lightning: Cracking Open the Writer's Craft*. New York: Bantam Books. (Also available on audio tape, which we recommend.)

Grabhorn, Lynn. 2000. *Excuse Me, Your Life Is Waiting*. Charlottesville, Virginia: Hampton Roads.

Hicks, Esther and Jerry. 2004. *Ask and It Is Given: Learning to Manifest Your Desires*. Carlsbad, California: Hay House.

Kingston, Karen. 1999. *Clear Your Clutter with Feng Shui*. New York: Broadway Books.

Klauser, Henriette Anne. 2000. *Write It Down, Make It Happen*. New York: Scribner.

Lamott, Anne. 1994. *Bird by Bird: Some Instructions on Writing and Life*. New York: Pantheon Books.

McTaggart, Lynne. 2002. *The Field: The Quest for the Secret Force of the Universe*. New York: Harper Collins.

Newton, Sir Isaac. 1999. *The Principia: Mathematical Principles of Natural Philosophy. A New Translation* by I. Bernard Cohen and Anne Whitman, assisted by Julia Budenz. Berkeley: University of California Press.

Sher, Barbara. 2004. *Wishcraft: How to Get What You Really Want*. New York: Ballantine Books.

Write Free

About the Authors

Rebecca Lawton's essays about life on wild rivers, *Reading Water: Lessons from the River* (Capital Books), was a ForeWord Nature Book of the Year finalist and was excerpted in *The Best Women's Travel Writing 2006* (Travelers Tales). She co-authored *Discover Nature in the Rocks* (Stackpole Books) and *On Foot in Sonoma* (Kulupi Press). Her literary honors include the Ellen Meloy Fund Award for Desert Writers. Her essays, poetry, and stories have been published in *Orion,*  *Sierra, The San Francisco Chronicle Magazine,* and many other journals. She holds an MFA in literature and creative writing from Mills College. Her work is available online at: www.beccalawton.com.

Visit Rebecca and Jordan at: www.writefree.us

Jordan E. Rosenfeld is a novelist, freelance writer, author of *Make a Scene: How to Craft a Powerful Story One Scene at a Time* (Writer's Digest Books), and editor of the anthology Zebulon Nights (Word Riot Press, 2002). She  is a contributing editor to *Writer's Digest* magazine, a book reviewer for KQED Radio, and has been published in *The San Francisco Chronicle, The St. Petersburg Times, Marin* magazine, Alternet. org, and many others. She holds an MFA in literature and creative writing from Bennington College. Her work is available online at: www.jordanrosenfeld.net.